I0541385

FROM
THE RANKS

CAPT. CHARLES KING

1st WORLD
LIBRARY
Literary Society

From the Ranks

Charles King

© 1st World Library, 2007
PO Box 2211
Fairfield, IA 52556
www.1stworldlibrary.com
First Edition

LCCN: 2007930723

Softcover ISBN: 978-1-4218-4803-7
Hardcover ISBN: 978-1-4218-4706-1
eBook ISBN: 978-1-4218-4900-3

Purchase *"From the Ranks"*
as a traditional bound book at:
www.1stWorldLibrary.com/purchase.asp?ISBN=978-1-4218-4803-7

1st World Library is a literary, educational organization
dedicated to:

- Creating a free internet library of downloadable ebooks

- Hosting writing competitions and offering book publishing
  scholarships.

Interested in more 1st World Library books? contact:
literacy@1stworldlibrary.com
Check us out at: www.1stworldlibrary.com

1ˢᵗ World Library Literary Society

Giving Back to the World

"If you want to work on the core problem, it's early school literacy."

- James Barksdale, former CEO of Netscape

"No skill is more crucial to the future of a child, or to a democratic and prosperous society, than literacy."

- Los Angeles Times

"Literacy... means far more than learning how to read and write... The aim is to transmit... knowledge and promote social participation."

- UNESCO

"Literacy is not a luxury, it is a right and a responsibility. If our world is to meet the challenges of the twenty-first century we must harness the energy and creativity of all our citizens."

- President Bill Clinton

"Parents should be encouraged to read to their children, and teachers should be equipped with all available techniques for teaching literacy, so the varying needs and capacities of individual kids can be taken into account."

- Hugh Mackay

I

A strange thing had happened at the old fort during the still watches of the night. Even now, at nine in the morning, no one seemed to be in possession of the exact circumstances. The officer of the day was engaged in an investigation, and all that appeared to be generally known was the bald statement that the sentry on "Number Five" had fired at somebody or other about half after three; that he had fired by order of the officer of the day, who was on his post at the time; and that now he flatly refused to talk about the matter.

Garrison curiosity, it is perhaps needless to say, was rather stimulated than lulled by this announcement. An unusual number of officers were chatting about head-quarters when Colonel Maynard came over to his office. Several ladies, too, who had hitherto shown but languid interest in the morning music of the band, had taken the trouble to stroll down to the old quadrangle, ostensibly to see guard-mounting. Mrs. Maynard was almost always on her piazza at this time, and her lovely daughter was almost sure to be at the gate with two or three young fellows lounging about her. This morning, however, not a soul appeared in front of the colonel's quarters.

Guard-mounting at the fort was not held until nine o'clock, contrary to the somewhat general custom at other posts in our scattered army. Colonel Maynard had ideas of his own upon the subject, and it was his theory that everything worked more smoothly if he had finished a leisurely breakfast before beginning office-work of any kind, and neither the colonel nor his family cared to breakfast before eight o'clock. In view of the fact that Mrs. Maynard had borne that name but a very short time and that her knowledge of army life dated only from the month of May, the garrison was disposed to consider her entitled to much latitude of choice in such matters, even while it did say that she was old enough to be above bride-like sentiment. The womenfolk at the fort were of opinion that Mrs. Maynard was fifty. It must be conceded that she was over forty, also that this was her second entry into the bonds of matrimony.

That no one should now appear on the colonel's piazza was obviously a disappointment to several people. In some way or other most of the breakfast tables at the post had been enlivened by accounts of the mysterious shooting. The soldiers going the rounds with the "police-cart," the butcher and grocer and baker from town, the old milkwoman with her glistening cans, had all served as newsmongers from kitchen to kitchen, and the story that came in with the coffee to the lady of the house had lost nothing in bulk or bravery. The groups of officers chatting and smoking in front of head-quarters gained accessions every moment, while the ladies seemed more absorbed in chat and confidences than in the sweet music of the band.

What fairly exasperated some men was the fact that the old officer of the day was not out on the parade where he belonged. Only the new incumbent was standing there in statuesque pose as the band trooped along the line, and the fact that the colonel had sent out word that the ceremony would proceed without Captain Chester only served to add fuel to the flame of popular conjecture. It was known that the colonel was holding a consultation with closed doors with the old officer of the day, and never before since he came to the regiment had the colonel been known to look so pale and strange as when he glanced out for just one moment and called his orderly. The soldier sprang up, saluted, received his message, and, with every eye following him, sped off towards the old stone guard-house. In three minutes he was on his way back, accompanied by a corporal and private of the guard in full dress uniform.

"That's Leary,—the man who fired the shot," said Captain Wilton to his senior lieutenant, who stood by his side.

"Belongs to B Company, doesn't he?" queried the subaltern. "Seems to me I have heard Captain Armitage say he was one of his best men."

"Yes. He's been in the regiment as long as I can remember. What on earth can the colonel want him for? Near as I can learn, he only fired by Chester's order."

"And neither of them knows what he fired at."

It was perhaps ten minutes more before Private Leary came forth from the door-way of the colonel's office, nodded to the corporal, and, raising their white-gloved hands in salute to the group of officers, the two men tossed their rifles to the right shoulder and strode back to the guard.

Another moment, and the colonel himself opened his door and appeared in the hall-way. He stopped abruptly, turned back and spoke a few words in low tone, then hurried through the groups at the entrance, looking at no man, avoiding their glances, and giving faint and impatient return to the soldierly salutations that greeted him. The sweat was beaded on his forehead; his lips were white, and his face full of a trouble and dismay no man had ever seen there before. He spoke to no one, but walked rapidly homeward, entered, and closed the gate and door behind him.

For a moment there was silence in the group. Few men in the service were better loved and honored than the veteran soldier who commanded the—th Infantry; and it was with genuine concern that his officers saw him so deeply and painfully affected,—for affected he certainly was. Never before had his cheery voice denied them a cordial "Good-morning, gentlemen." Never before had his blue eyes flinched. He had been their comrade and commander in years of frontier service, and his bachelor home had been the rendezvous of all genial spirits when in garrison. They had missed him sorely when he went abroad on long leave the previous year, and were almost indignant when they received the news that he had met his fate in Italy and would return married. "She" was the widow of a wealthy New-Yorker who had been dead some three years only, and, though over forty, did not look her years to masculine eyes when she reached the fort in May. After knowing her a week, the garrison had decided to a man that the colonel had done wisely. Mrs. Maynard was charming, courteous, handsome, and accomplished. Only among the women were there still a few who resented their colonel's capture; and some of these, oblivious of the fact that they had tempted him with relations of their own, were sententious and severe in their condem-nation of second marriage; for the colonel, too, was indulging in a second experiment. Of his first, only one man in the regiment, besides the commander, could tell anything; and he, to the just indignation of almost everybody, would not discuss the subject. It was rumored that in the old days when Maynard was senior captain and Chester junior subaltern in their former regiment the two had very little in common. It was known that the first Mrs. Maynard, while still young and beautiful, had died abroad. It was hinted that the resignation of a dashing lieutenant of the regiment, which was synchronous with her departure for foreign shores, was demanded by his brother officers; but it was useless asking Captain Chester. He could not tell; and—wasn't it odd?— here was Chester again, the only man in the colonel's confidence in an hour of evident trouble.

"By Jove! what's gone wrong with the chief?" was the first exclamation from one of the older officers. "I never saw him look so broken."

As no explanation suggested itself, they began edging in towards the office. The door stood open; a hand-bell banged; a clerk darted in from the sergeant-major's rooms, and Captain Chester was revealed seated at the colonel's desk. This in itself was sufficient to induce several officers to stroll in and look inquiringly around. Captain Chester, merely nodding, went on with some writing at which he was engaged.

After a moment's awkward silence and uneasy glancing at one another, the party seemed to arrive at the conclusion that it was time to speak. The band had ceased, and the new guard had marched away behind its pealing bugles. Lieutenant Hall winked at his comrades, strolled hesitatingly over to the desk, balanced unsteadily on one leg, and, with his hands sticking in his trousers-pockets and his forage-cap swinging from protruding thumb and forefinger, cleared his throat, and, with marked lack of confidence, accosted his absorbed superior:

"Colonel gone home?"

"Didn't you see him?" was the uncompromising reply; and the captain did not deign to raise his head or eyes.

"Well—er—yes, I suppose I did," said Mr. Hall, shifting uncomfortably to his other leg, and prodding the floor with the toe of his boot.

"Then that wasn't what you wanted to know, I presume," said Captain Chester, signing his name with a vicious dab of the pen and bringing his fist down with a thump on the blotting-pad, while he wheeled around in his chair and looked squarely up into the perturbed features of the junior.

"No, it wasn't," answered Mr. Hall, in an injured tone, while an audible snicker at the door added to his sense of discomfort. "What I mainly wanted was to know could I go to town."

"That matter is easily arranged, Mr. Hall. All you have to do is to get out of that uncomfortable and unsoldierly position, stand in the attitude in which you are certainly more at home and infinitely more picturesque, proffer your request in respectful words, and there is no question as to the result."

"Oh! you're in command, then?" said Mr. Hall, slowly wriggling into the position of the soldier and flushing through his bronzed cheeks. "I thought the colonel might be only gone for a minute."

"The colonel may not be back for a week; but you be here for dress-parade all the same, and—Mr. Hall!" he called, as the young officer was turning away. The latter faced about again.

"Was Mr. Jerrold going with you to town?"

"Yes, sir. He was to drive me in his dog-cart, and it's over here now."

"Mr. Jerrold cannot go,—at least not until I have seen him."

"Why, captain, he got the colonel's permission at breakfast this morning."

"That is true, no doubt, Mr. Hall." And the captain dropped his sharp and captious manner, and his voice fell, as though in sympathy with the cloud that settled on his face. "I cannot explain matters just now. There are reasons why the permission is withdrawn for the time being. The adjutant will notify him." And Captain Chester turned to his desk again as the new officer of the day, guard-book in hand, entered to make his report.

"The usual orders, captain," said Chester, as he took the book from his hand and looked over the list of prisoners. Then, in bold and rapid strokes, he wrote across the page the customary certificate of the old officer of the day, winding up with this remark:

"He also inspected guard and visited sentries between 3 and 3.35 a.m. The firing at 3.30 a.m. was by his order."

Meantime, those officers who had entered and who had no immediate duty to perform were standing or seated around the room, but all observing profound silence. For a moment or two no sound was heard but the scratching of the captain's pen. Then, with some embarrassment and hesitancy, he laid it down and glanced around him.

"Has any one here anything to ask,—any business to transact?"

Two or three mentioned some routine matters that required the action of the post-commander, but did so reluctantly, as though they preferred to await the orders of the colonel himself. Captain Wilton, indeed, spoke his sentiments:

"I wanted to see Colonel Maynard about getting two men of my company relieved from extra duty; but, as he isn't here, I fancy I had better wait."

"Not at all. Who are your men?—Have it done at once, Mr. Adjutant, and supply their places from my company, if need be. Now is there anything else?"

The group was apparently "nonplussed," as the adjutant afterwards put it, by such unlooked-for complaisance on the part of the usually crotchety senior captain. Still, no one offered to lead the others and leave the room. After a moment's nervous rapping with his knuckles on the desk, Captain Chester again abruptly spoke:

"Gentlemen, I am sorry to incommode you, but, if there be nothing more that you desire to see me about, I shall go on with some other matters, which—pardon me—do not require your presence."

At this very broad hint the party slowly found their legs, and with much wonderment and not a few resentful glances at their temporary commander the officers sauntered to the door-way. There, however, several stopped again, still reluctant to leave in the face of so pervading a mystery, for Wilton turned.

"Am I to understand that Colonel Maynard has left the post to be gone any length of time?" he asked.

"He has not yet gone. I do not know how long he will be gone or how soon he will start. For pressing personal reasons he has turned over the command to me; and, if he decide to remain away, of course some field-officer will be ordered to come to head-quarters. For a day or two you will have to worry along with me; but I shan't worry you more than I can help. I've got mystery and mischief enough here to keep me busy, God knows. Just ask Sloat to come back here to me, will you? And—Wilton, I did not mean to be abrupt with you. I'm all upset to-day. Mr. Adjutant, notify Mr. Jerrold at once that he must not leave the post until I have seen him. It is the colonel's last order. Tell him so."

II

The night before had been unusually dark. A thick veil of clouds overspread the heavens and hid the stars. Moon there was none, for the faint silver crescent that gleamed for a moment through the swift-sailing wisps of vapor had dropped beneath the horizon soon after tattoo, and the mournful strains of "taps," borne on the rising wind, seemed to signal "extinguish lights" to the entire firmament as well as to Fort Sibley. There was a dance of some kind at the quarters of one of the staff-officers living far up the row on the southern terrace. Chester heard the laughter and chat as the young officers and their convoy of matrons and maids came tripping homeward after midnight. He was a crusty old bachelor, to use his own description, and rarely ventured into these scenes of social gayety, and, besides, he was officer of the day, and it was a theory he was fond of expounding to juniors that when on guard no soldier should permit himself to be drawn from the scene of his duties. With his books and his pipe Chester whiled away the lonely hours of the early night, and wondered if the wind would blow up a rain or disperse the clouds entirely. Towards one o'clock a light, bounding footstep approached his door, and the portal flew open as a trim-built young fellow with laughing eyes and an air of exuberant health and spirits came briskly in. It was Rollins, the junior second lieutenant of the regiment, and Chester's own and only pet,—so said the envious others. He was barely a year out of leading-strings at the Point, and as full of hope and pluck and mischief as a colt. Moreover, he was frank and teachable, said Chester, and didn't come to him with the idea that he had nothing to learn and less to do. The boy won upon his gruff captain from the very start, and, to the incredulous delight of the whole regiment, within six months the old cynic had taken him into his heart and home, and Mr. Rollins occupied a pleasant room under Chester's roof-tree, and was the sole accredited sharer of the captain's mess. To a youngster just entering service, whose ambition it was to stick to business and make a record for zeal and efficiency, these were manifest advantages. There were men in the regiment to whom such close communion with a watchful senior would have been most embarrassing, and Mr. Rollins's predecessor as second lieutenant of Chester's company was one of these. Mr. Jerrold was a happy man when promotion took him from under the wing of "Crusty Jake" and landed him in Company B. More than that, it came just at a time when, after four years of loneliness and isolation at an up-river stockade, his new company and his old one, together with four others from the regiment, were ordered to join head-quarters and the band at the most delightful station in the Northwest. Here Mr. Rollins had reported for duty during the previous autumn, and here they were with troops of other arms of the service, enjoying the close proximity of all the good things of civilization.

Chester looked up with a quizzical smile as his "plebe" came in:

"Well, sir, how many dances had you with 'Sweet Alice, Ben Bolt'? Not many, I fancy, with Mr. Jerrold monopolizing everything, as usual. By gad! some good fellow could make a colossal fortune in buying that young man at my valuation and selling him at his own."

"Oh, come, now, captain," laughed Rollins, "Jerrold's no such slouch as you make him out. He's lazy, and he likes to spoon, and he puts up with a good deal of petting from the girls,—who wouldn't, if he could get it?—but he is jolly and big-hearted, and don't put on any airs,—with us, at least,—and the mess like him first-rate. 'Tain't his fault that he's handsome and a regular lady-killer. You must admit that he had a pretty tough four years of it up there at that cussed old Indian graveyard, and it's only natural he should enjoy getting here, where there are theatres and concerts and operas and dances and dinners—"

"Yes, dances and dinners and daughters,—all delightful, I know, but no excuse for a man's neglecting his manifest duty, as he is doing and has been ever since we got here. Any other time the colonel would have straightened him out; but no use trying it now, when both women in his household are as big fools about the man as anybody in town,—bigger, unless I'm a born idiot." And Chester rose excitedly.

"I suppose he had Miss Renwick pretty much to himself to-night?" he presently demanded, looking angrily and searchingly at his junior, as though half expecting him to dodge the question.

"Oh, yes. Why not? It's pretty evident she would rather dance and be with him than with any one else: so what can a fellow do? Of course we ask her to dance, and all that, and I think he wants us to; but I cannot help feeling rather a bore to her, even if she is only eighteen, and there are plenty of pleasant girls in the garrison who don't get any too much attention, now we're so near a big city, and I like to be with them."

"Yes, and it's the *right* thing for you to do, youngster. That's one trait I despise in Jerrold. When we were up there at the stockade two winters ago, and Captain Gray's little girl was there, he hung around her from morning till night, and the poor little thing fairly beamed and blossomed with delight. Look at her now, man! He don't go near her. He hasn't had the decency to take her a walk, a drive, or anything, since we got here. He began, from the moment we came, with that gang in town. He was simply devoted to Miss Beaubien until Alice Renwick came; then he dropped her like a hot brick. By the Eternal, Rollins, he hasn't gotten off with *that* old love yet, you mark my words. There's Indian blood in her veins, and a look in her eye that makes me wriggle, sometimes. I watched her last night at parade when she drove out here with that copper-faced old squaw, her mother. For all her French and Italian education and her years in New York and Paris, that girl's got a wild streak in her somewhere. She sat there watching him as the officers marched to the front, and then *her*, as he went up and joined Miss Renwick; and there was a gleam of her white teeth and a flash in her black eyes that made me think of the leap of a knife from the sheath. Not but what 'twould serve him right if she did play him some devil's trick. It's his own doing. Were any people out from town?" he suddenly asked.

"Yes, half a dozen or so," answered Mr. Rollins, who was pulling off his boots and inserting his feet into easy slippers, while old "Crusty" tramped excitedly up and down the floor. "Most of them stayed out here, I think. Only one team went back across the bridge."

"Whose was that?"

"The Suttons', I believe. Young Cub Sutton was out with his sister and another girl."

"There's another damned fool!" growled Chester. "That boy has ten thousand a year of his own, a beautiful home that will be his, a doting mother and sister, and everything wealth can buy, and yet, by gad! he's unhappy because he can't be a poor devil of a lieutenant, with nothing but drills, debts, and rifle-practice to enliven him. That's what brings him out here all the time. He'd swap places with you in a minute. Isn't he very thick with Jerrold?"

"Oh, yes, rather. Jerrold entertains him a good deal."

"Which is returned with compound interest, I'll bet you. Mr. Jerrold simply makes a convenience of him. He won't make love to his sister, because the poor, rich, unsophisticated girl is as ugly as she is ubiquitous. His majesty is fastidious, you see, and seeks only the caress of beauty, and while he lives there at the Suttons' when he goes to town, and dines and sleeps and smokes and wines there, and uses their box at the opera-house, and is courted and flattered by the old lady because dear Cubby worships the ground he walks on and poor Fanny Sutton thinks him adorable, he turns his back on the girl at every dance because she *can't* dance, and leaves her to you fellows who have a conscience and some idea of decency. He gives all *his* devotions to Nina Beaubien, who dances like a *coryphee*, and drops *her* when Alice Renwick comes with her glowing Spanish beauty. Oh, damn it, I'm an old fool to get worked up over it as I do, but you young fellows don't see what I see. You haven't seen what I've seen; and pray God you never may! That's where the shoe pinches, Rollins. It is what he *reminds* me of—not so much what he *is*, I suppose—that I get rabid about. He is for all the world like a man we had in the old regiment when you were in swaddling-clothes; and I never look at Mamie Gray's sad, white face that it doesn't bring back a girl I knew just then whose heart was broken by just such a shallow, selfish, adorable scoun—No, I won't use *that* word in speaking of Jerrold; but it's what I fear. Rollins, you call him generous. Well, so he is,—*lavish*, if you like, with his money and his hospitality here in the post. Money comes easily to him, and goes; but you boys misuse the term. *I* call him selfish to the core, because he can deny himself no luxury, no pleasure, though it may wring a woman's life—or, more than that, her honor—to give it him." The captain was tramping up and down the room now, as was his wont when excited; his face was flushed, and his hand clinched. He turned suddenly and faced the younger officer, who sat gazing uncomfortably at the rug in front of the fireplace.

"Rollins, some day I may tell you a story that I've kept to myself all these years. You won't wonder at my feeling as I do about these goings-on of your friend Jerrold when you hear it all, but it was just such a man as he who ruined one woman, broke the heart of another, and took the sunshine out of the life of two men from that day to this. One of them was your colonel, the other your captain. Now go to bed. I'm going out." And, throwing down his pipe, regardless of the scattering sparks and ashes, Captain Chester strode into the hall-way, picked up the first forage-cap he laid hands on, and banged himself out of the front door.

Mr. Rollins remained for some moments in the same attitude, still gazing abstractedly at the rug, and listening to the nervous tramp of his senior officer on the piazza without. Then he slowly and thoughtfully went to his room, where his perturbed spirit was soon soothed in sleep. His conscience being clear and his health perfect, there were no deep cares to keep him tossing on a restless pillow.

To Chester, however, sleep was impossible: he tramped the piazza a full hour before he felt placid enough to go and inspect his guard. The sentries were calling three o'clock, and the wind had died away, as he started on his round. Dark as was the night, he carried no lantern. The main garrison was well lighted by lamps, and the road circling the old fort was broad, smooth, and bordered by a stone coping wall where it skirted the precipitous descent into the river-bottom. As he passed down the plank walk west of the quadrangle wherein lay the old barracks and the stone quarters of the commanding officer and the low one-storied row of bachelor dens, he could not help noting the silence and peace of the night. Not a light was visible at any window as he strode down the line. The challenge of the sentry at the old stone tower sounded unnecessarily sharp and loud, and his response of "Officer of the day" was lower than usual, as though rebuking the unseemly outcry. The guard came scrambling out and formed hurriedly to receive him, but the captain's inspection was of the briefest kind. Barely glancing along the prison corridor to see that the bars were in place, he turned back into the night, and made for the line of posts along the river-bank. The sentry at the high bridge across the gorge, and the next one, well around to the southeast flank, were successively visited and briefly questioned as to their instructions, and then the captain plodded sturdily on until he came to the sharp bend around the outermost angle of the fort and found himself passing behind the quarters of the commanding officer, a substantial two-storied stone house with mansard roof and dormer-windows. The road in the rear was some ten feet below the level of the parade inside the quadrangle, and consequently, as the house faced the parade, what was the ground-floor from that front became the second story at the rear. The kitchen, store-room, and servants' rooms were on this lower stage, and opened upon the road; an outer stairway ran up to the centre door at the back, but at the east and west flanks of the house the stone walls stood without port or window except those above the eaves,—the dormers. Light and air in abundance streamed through the broad Venetian windows north and south when light and air were needed. This night, as usual, all was tightly closed below, all darkness aloft as he glanced up at the dormers high above his head. As he did so, his foot struck a sudden and sturdy obstacle; he stumbled and pitched heavily forward, and found himself sprawling at full length upon a ladder lying on the ground almost in the middle of the roadway.

"Damn those painters!" he growled between his set teeth. "They leave their infernal man-traps around in the very hope of catching me, I believe. Now, who but a painter would have left a ladder in such a place as this?"

Rising ruefully and rubbing a bruised knee with his hand, he limped painfully ahead a few steps, until he came to the side-wall of the colonel's house. Here a plank walk passed from the roadway along the western wall until almost on a line with the front piazza, where by a flight of steps it was carried up to the level of the parade. Here he paused a moment to dust off his clothes and rearrange his belt and sword. He stood leaning against the wall and facing the gray stone gable end of the row of old-fashioned quarters that bounded the parade upon the southwest. All was still darkness and silence.

"Confound this sword!" he muttered again: "the thing made rattle and racket enough to wake the dead. Wonder if I disturbed anybody at the colonel's."

As though in answer to his suggestion, there suddenly appeared, high on the blank wall before him, the reflection of a faint light. Had a little night-lamp been turned on in the front room of the upper story? The gleam came from the north window on the side: he saw plainly the shadow of the pretty lace curtains, looped loosely back. Then the shade was gently raised, and there was for an instant the silhouette of a slender hand and wrist, the shadow of a lace-bordered sleeve. Then the light receded, as though carried back across the room, waned, as though slowly extinguished, and the last shadows showed the curtains still looped back, the rolling shade still raised.

"I thought so," he growled. "One tumble like that is enough to wake the Seven Sleepers, let alone a love-sick girl who is probably dreaming over Jerrold's parting words. She is spirited and blue-blooded enough to have more sense, too, that same superb brunette. Ah, Miss Alice, I wonder if you think that fellow's love worth having. It is two hours since he left you,—more than that,—and here you are awake yet,—cannot sleep,—want more air, and have to come and raise your shade. No such warm night, either." These were his reflections as he picked up his offending sword and, more slowly and cautiously now, groped his way along the western terrace. He passed the row of bachelor quarters, and was well out beyond the limits of the fort before he came upon the next sentry,—"Number Five,"—and recognized, in the stern "Who comes there?" and the sharp rattle of the bayonet as it dropped to the charge, the well-known challenge of Private Leary, one of the oldest and most reliable soldiers in the regiment.

"All right on your post, Leary?" he asked, after having given the countersign.

"All right, I *think*, sor; though if the captain had asked me that half an hour ago I'd not have said so. It was so dark I couldn't see me hand afore me face, sor; but about half-past two I was walkin' very slow down back of the quarters, whin just close by Loot'nant Jerrold's back gate I seen somethin' movin', and as I come softly along it riz up, an' sure I thought 'twas the loot'nant himself, whin he seemed to catch sight o' me or hear me, and he backed inside the gate an' shut it. I was sure 'twas he, he was so tall and slim like, an' so I niver said a word until I got to thinkin' over it, and then I couldn't spake. Sure if it had been the loot'nant he wouldn't have backed away from a sintry; he'd 'a' come out bold and given the countersign; but I didn't think o' that. It looked like him in the dark, an' 'twas his quarters, an' I thought it *was* him, until I thought ag'in, and then, sor, I wint back and searched the yard; but there was no one there."

"Hm! Odd thing that, Leary! Why didn't you challenge at first?"

"Sure, sor, he lept inside the fince quick as iver we set eyes on each other. He was bendin' down, and I thought it was one of the hound pups when I first sighted him."

"And he hasn't been around since?"

"No, sor, nor nobody, till the officer of the day came along."

Chester walked away puzzled. Sibley was a most quiet and orderly garrison. Night prowlers had never been heard from, especially over here at the south and southwest fronts. The enlisted men going to or from town passed across the big, high bridge or went at once to their own quarters on the east and north. This southwestern terrace behind the bachelors' row was the most secluded spot on the whole post,—so much so that when a fire broke out there among the fuel-heaps one sharp winter's night a year agone it had wellnigh enveloped the whole line before its existence was discovered. Indeed, not until after this occurrence was a sentry posted on that front at all; and, once ordered there, he had so little to do and was so comparatively sure to be undisturbed that the old soldiers eagerly sought the post in preference to any other, and were given it as a peace privilege. For months, relief after relief tramped around the fort and found the terrace post as humdrum and silent as an empty church; but this night "Number Five" leaped suddenly into notoriety.

Instead of going home, Chester kept on across the plateau and took a long walk on the northern side of the reservation, where the quarter-master's stables and corrals were placed. He was affected by a strange unrest. His talk with Rollins had roused the memories of years long gone by,—of days when he, too, was young and full of hope and faith, ay, full of love,—all lavished on one fair girl who knew it well, but gently, almost entreatingly, repelled him. Her heart was wrapped up in another, the Adonis of his day in the gay old seaboard garrison. She was a soldier's child, barrack-born, simply taught, knowing little of the vice and temptations, the follies and the frauds, of the whirling life of civilization. A good and gentle mother had reared her and been called hence. Her father, an officer whose sabre-arm was left at Molino del Rey, and whose heart was crushed when the loving wife was taken from him, turned to the child who so resembled her, and centred there all his remaining love and life. He welcomed Chester to his home, and tacitly favored his suit, but in his blindness never saw how a few moonlit strolls on the old moss-grown parapet, a few evening dances in the casemates with handsome, wooing, winning Will Forrester, had done their work. She gave him all the wild, enthusiastic, worshipping love of her girlish heart just about the time Captain and Mrs. Maynard came back from leave, and then he grew cold and negligent *there*, but lived at Maynard's fireside; and one day there came a sensation,—a tragedy,—and Mrs. Maynard went away, and died abroad, and a shocked and broken-hearted girl hid her face from all and pined at home, and Mr. Forrester's resignation was sent from—no one knew just where, and no one would have cared to know, except Maynard. He would have followed him, pistol in hand, but Forrester gave him no chance. Years afterwards Chester again sought her and offered her his love and his name. It was useless, she told him, sadly. She lived only for her father now, and would never leave him till he died, and then—she prayed she might go too. Memories like

Charles King

this *will* come up at such times in these same "still watches of the night." Chester was in a moody frame of mind when about half an hour later he came back past the guard-house. The sergeant was standing near the lighted entrance, and the captain called him:

"There's a ladder lying back of the colonel's quarters on the roadway. Some of those painters left it, I suppose. It's a wonder some of the reliefs have not broken their necks over it going around to-night. Let the next one pick it up and move it out of the way. Hasn't it been reported?"

"Not to me, sir. Corporal Schreiber has command of this relief, and he has said nothing about it. Here he is, sir."

"Didn't you see it or stumble over it when posting your relief, corporal?" asked Chester.

"No indeed, sir. I—I think the captain must have been mistaken in thinking it a ladder. We would surely have struck it if it had been."

"No mistake at all, corporal. I lifted it. It is a long, heavy ladder,—over twenty feet, I should say."

"There *is* such a ladder back there, captain," said the sergeant, "but it always hangs on the fence just behind the young officers' quarters,—Bachelors' Row, sir, I mean."

"And that ladder was there an hour ago when I went my rounds," said the corporal, earnestly. "I had my hurricane-lamp, sir, and saw it on the fence plainly. And there was nothing behind the colonel's at that hour."

Chester turned away, thoughtful and silent. Without a word he walked straight into the quadrangle, past the low line of stone buildings, the offices of the adjutant and quartermaster, the home of the sergeant-major, the club and billiard-room, past the long, piazza-shaded row of bachelor quarters, and came upon the plank walk at the corner of the colonel's fence. Ten more steps, and he stood stock-still at the head of the flight of wooden stairs.

There, dimly visible against the southern sky, its base on the plank walk below him, its top resting upon the eaves midway between the dormer-window and the roof of the piazza, so that one could step easily from it into the one or on to the other, was the very ladder that half an hour before was lying on the ground behind the house.

His heart stood still. He seemed powerless to move,—even to think. Then a slight noise roused him, and with every nerve tingling he crouched ready for a spring. With quick, agile movements, noiseless as a cat, sinuous and stealthy as a serpent, the dark figure of a man issued from Alice Renwick's chamber window and came gliding down.

One second more, and, almost as noiselessly, he reached the ground, then quickly raised and turned the ladder, stepped with it to the edge of the roadway, and peered around the angle as though to see that no sentry was in sight, then vanished with his burden around the corner. Another second, and down the steps went Chester, three at a bound, tip-toeing it in pursuit. Ten seconds brought him close to the culprit,— a tall, slender shadow.

"You villain! Halt!"

Down went the ladder on the dusty road. The hand that Chester had clinched upon the broad shoulder was hurled aside. There was a sudden whirl, a lightning blow that took the captain full in the chest and staggered him back upon the treacherous and entangling rungs, and, ere he could recover himself, the noiseless stranger had fairly whizzed into space and vanished in the darkness up the road. Chester sprang in pursuit. He heard the startled challenge of the sentry, and then Leary's excited "Halt, I say! Halt!" and then he shouted,—

"Fire on him, Leary! Bring him down!"

Bang went the ready rifle with sharp, sullen roar that woke the echoes across the valley. Bang again, as Leary sent a second shot after the first. Then, as the captain came panting to the spot, they followed up the road. No sign of the runner. Attracted by the shots, the sergeant of the guard and one or two men, lantern-bearing, came running to the scene. Excitedly they searched up and down the road in mingled hope and dread of finding the body of the marauder, or some clue or trace. Nothing! Whoever he was, the fleet runner had vanished and made good his escape.

"Who could it have been, sir?" asked the sergeant of the officer of the day. "Surely none of the men ever come round this way."

"I don't know, sergeant; I don't know. Just take your lamp and see if there is anything visible down there among the rocks. He may have been hit and leaped the wall.—Do you think you hit him, Leary?"

"I can't say, sor. He came by me like a flash. I had just a second's look at him, and—Sure I niver saw such runnin'."

"Could you see his face?" asked Chester, in a low tone, as the other men moved away to search the rocks.

"Not his face, sor. 'Twas too dark."

"Was there—did he look like anybody you knew, or had seen?—anybody in the command?"

"Well, sor, not among the men, that is. There's none so tall and slim both, and so light. Sure he must 'a' worn gums, sor. You couldn't hear the whisper of a footfall."

"But whom did he *seem* to resemble?"

"Well, if the captain will forgive me, sor, it's unwillin' I am to say the worrd, but there's no one that tall and light and slim here, sor, but Loot'nant Jerrold. Sure it couldn't be him, sor."

"Leary, will you promise me something on your word as a man?"

"I will, sor."

"Say not one word of this matter to any one, except I tell you, or you have to, before a court."

"I promise, sor."

"And I believe you. Tell the sergeant I will soon be back."

With that he turned and walked down the road until once more he came to the plank crossing and the passage-way between the colonel's and Bachelors' Row. Here again he stopped short, and waited with bated breath and scarcely-beating heart. The faint light he had seen before again illumined the room and cast its gleam upon the old gray wall. Even as he gazed, there came silently to the window a tall, white-robed form, and a slender white hand seized and lowered the shade, noiselessly. Then, as before, the light faded away; but—she was awake.

Waiting one moment in silence, Captain Chester then sprang up the wooden steps and passed under the piazza which ran the length of the bachelor quarters. Half-way down the row he turned sharply to his left, opened the green-painted door, and stood in a little dark hall-way. Taking his match-box from his pocket, he struck a light, and by its glare quickly read the card upon the first door-way to his right:

"MR. HOWARD F. JERROLD,

"—*th Infantry, U.S.A.*"

Opening this door, he bolted straight through the little parlor to the bedroom in the rear. A dim light was burning on the mantel. The bed was unruffled, untouched, and Mr. Jerrold was not there.

Five minutes afterwards, Captain Chester, all alone, had laboriously and cautiously dragged the ladder from the side to the rear of the colonel's house, stretched it in the roadway where he had first stumbled upon it, then returned to the searching-party on "Number Five."

"Send two men to put that ladder back," he ordered. "It is where I told you,—on the road behind the colonel's."

III

When Mrs. Maynard came to Sibley in May and the officers with their wives were making their welcoming call, she had with motherly pride and pleasure yielded to their constant importunities and shown to one party after another an album of photographs,—likenesses of her only daughter. There were little *cartes de visite* representing her in long dresses and baby-caps; quaint little pictures of a chubby-faced, chubby-legged infant a few months older; charming studies of a little girl with great black eyes and delicate features; then of a tall, slender slip of a maiden, decidedly foreign-looking; then of a sweet and pensive face, with great dark eyes, long, beautiful curling lashes, and very heavy, low-arched brows, exquisitely moulded mouth and chin, and most luxuriant dark hair; then others, still older, in every variety of dress,—even in fancy costume, such as the girl had worn at fair or masquerade. These and others still had Mrs. Maynard shown them, with repressed pride and pleasure and with sweet acknowledgment of their enthusiastic praises. Alice still tarried in the East, visiting relatives whom she had not seen since her father's death three years earlier, and, long before she came to join her mother at Sibley and to enter upon the life she so eagerly looked forward to, "'way out in the West, you know, with officers and soldiers and the band, and buffalo and Indians all around you," there was not an officer or an officer's wife who had not delightedly examined that album. There was still another picture, but that one had been shown to only a chosen few just one week after her daughter's arrival, and rather an absurd scene had occurred, in which that most estimable officer, Lieutenant Sloat, had figured as the hero. A more simple-minded, well-intentioned fellow than Sloat there did not live. He was so full of kindness and good nature and readiness to do anything for anybody that it never seemed to occur to him that everybody on earth was not just as ready to be equally accommodating. He was a perpetual source of delight to the colonel, and one of the most loyal and devoted of subalterns, despite the fact that his locks were long silvered with the frosts of years and that he had fought through the war of the rebellion and risen to the rank of a field-officer in Maynard's old brigade. The most temperate of men, ordinarily, the colonel had one anniversary he loved to celebrate, and Sloat was his stand-by when the 3d of July came round, just as he had been at his shoulder at that supreme moment when, heedless of the fearful sweep of shell and canister through their shattered ranks, Pickett's heroic Virginians breasted the slope of Cemetery Hill and surged over the low stone wall into Cushing's guns. Hard, stubborn fighting had Maynard's men to do that day, and for serene courage and determination no man had beaten Sloat. Both officers had bullet-hole mementos to carry from that field; both had won their brevets for conspicuous gallantry, and Sloat was a happy and grateful man when, years afterwards, his old commander secured him a lieutenancy in the regular service. He was the colonel's henchman, although he never had brains enough to win a place on the regimental staff, and when Mrs. Maynard came he overwhelmed her with cumbrous compliments and incessant calls. He was, to his confident belief, her chosen and accepted knight for full two days after her arrival. Then Jerrold came back from a brief absence, and, as in duty bound, went to pay his respects to his colonel's wife; and that night there had been a singular scene. Mrs. Maynard had stopped suddenly in her laughing chat with two ladies, had started from her seat, wildly staring at the tall, slender subaltern who entered the gateway, and then fell back in her chair, fairly swooning as he made his bow.

Sloat had rushed into the house to call the colonel and get some water, while Mr. Jerrold stood paralyzed at so strange a reception of his first call. Mrs. Maynard revived presently, explained that it was her heart, or the heat, or something, and the ladies on their way home decided that it was possibly the heart, it was certainly not the heat, it was unquestionably something, and that something was Mr. Jerrold, for she never took her eyes off him during the entire evening, and seemed unable to shake off the fascination. Next day Jerrold dined there, and from that time on he was a daily visitor. Every one noted Mrs. Maynard's strong interest in him, but no one could account for it. She was old enough to be his mother, said the garrison; but not until Alice Renwick came did another consideration appear: he was singularly like the daughter. Both were tall, lithe, slender; both had dark, lustrous eyes, dark, though almost perfect, skin, exquisitely-chiselled features, and slender, shapely hands and feet. Alice was "the picture of her father," said Mrs. Maynard, and Mr. Renwick had lived all his life in New York; while Mr. Jerrold was of an old Southern family, and his mother a Cuban beauty who was the toast of the New Orleans clubs not many years before the war.

Poor Sloat! He did not fancy Jerrold, and was as jealous as so unselfish a mortal could be of the immediate ascendency the young fellow established in the colonel's household. It was bad enough before Alice joined them; after that it was wellnigh unbearable. Then came the 3d-of-July dinner and the colonel's one annual jollification. No man ever heard of Sloat's being intoxicated; he rarely drank at all; but this evening the reminiscences of the day, the generous wine, the unaccustomed elegance of all his surroundings, due to Mrs. Maynard's taste and supervision, and the influence of Alice Kenwick's exquisite beauty, had fairly carried him away.

They were chatting in the parlor, while Miss Renwick was entertaining some young-lady friends from town and listening to the band on the parade. Sloat was expatiating on her grace and beauty and going over the album for the twentieth time, when the colonel, with a twinkling eye, remarked to Mrs. Maynard,—

"I think you ought to show Major[A] Sloat the 'Directoire' picture, my dear."

"Alice would never forgive me," said madame, laughing; "though I consider it the most beautiful we have of her."

"Oh, where is it?" "Oh, do let us see it, Mrs. Maynard!" was the chorus of exclamations from the few ladies present. "Oh, I *insist* on seeing it, madame," was Sloat's characteristic contribution to the clamor.

"I want you to understand it," said Mrs. Maynard, pleased, but still hesitating. "We are very daft about Alice at home, you know, and it's quite a wonder she has not been utterly spoiled by her aunts and uncles; but this picture was a specialty. An artist friend of ours fairly *made* us have it taken in the wedding-dress worn by her grandmother. You know the Josephine Beauharnais 'Directoire' style that was worn in seventeen ninety-something. Her neck and shoulders are lovely, and that was why we consented. I went, and so did the artist, and we posed her, and the photograph is simply perfect of her face, and neck too, but when Alice saw it she blushed furiously and forbade my having them finished. Afterwards, though, she yielded when her aunt Kate and I begged so hard and promised that none should be given away, and so just half a dozen were finished. Indeed, the dress is by no means as *decollete* as many girls wear theirs at dinner now in New York; but poor Alice was scandalized when she saw it last month, and she never would let me put one in the album."

"Oh, *do* go and get it, Mrs. Maynard!" pleaded the ladies. "Oh, *please* let me see it, Mrs. Maynard!" added Sloat; and at last the mother-pride prevailed. Mrs. Maynard rustled upstairs, and presently returned holding in her hands a delicate silver frame in filigree-work, a quaint foreign affair, and enclosed therein was a cabinet photograph *en vignette*,—the head, neck, and shoulders of a beautiful girl; and the dainty, diminutive, what-there-was-of-it waist of the old-fashioned gown, sashed almost immediately under the exquisite bust, revealed quite materially the cause of Alice Renwick's blushes. But a more beautiful portrait was never photographed. The women fairly gasped with delight and envy. Sloat could not restrain his impatience to get it in his own hands, and finally he grasped it and then eyed it in rapture. It was two minutes before he spoke a word, while the colonel sat laughing at his worshipping gaze. Mrs. Maynard somewhat uneasily stretched forth her hand, and the other ladies impatiently strove to regain possession.

"Come, Major Sloat, you've surely had it long enough. *We* want it again."

"Never!" said Sloat, with melodramatic intensity. "Never! This is my ideal of perfection,—of divinity in woman. I will bear it home with me, set it above my fireside, and adore it day and night."

"Nonsense, Major Sloat!" said Mrs. Maynard, laughing, yet far from being at her ease. "Come, I *must* take it back. Alice may be in any minute now, and if she knew I had betrayed her she would never forgive me. Come, surrender!" And she strove to take it from him.

But Sloat was in one of his utterly asinine moods. He would have been perfectly willing to give any sum he possessed for so perfect a picture as this. He never dreamed that there were good and sufficient reasons why *no* man should have it. He so loved and honored his colonel that he was ready to lay down his life for any of his household. In laying claim to this picture he honestly believed that it was the highest proof he could give of his admiration and devotion. A tame surrender now meant that his protestations were empty words. "Therefore," argued Sloat, "I must stand firm."

"Madame," said he, "I'd die first." And with that he began backing to the door.

Alarmed now, Mrs. Maynard sprang after him, and the little major leaped upon a chair, his face aglow, jolly, rubicund, beaming with bliss and triumph. She looked up, almost wringing her hands, and turned half appealingly to the colonel, who was laughing heartily on the sofa, never dreaming Sloat could be in earnest.

"Here, I'll give you back the frame: I don't want that," said Sloat, and began fumbling at the back of the photograph. This was too much for the ladies. They, too, rushed to the rescue. One of them sprang to and shut the door, the other seized and violently shook the back of his chair, and Sloat leaped to the floor, still clinging to his prize, and laughing as though he had never had so much entertainment in his life. The long Venetian windows opened upon the piazza, and towards the nearest one he retreated, holding aloft the precious gage and waving off the attacking party with the other hand. He was within a yard of the blinds, when they were suddenly thrown open, a tall, slender form stepped quickly in, one hand seized the uplifted wrist, the other the picture, and in far less time than it takes to tell it Mr. Jerrold had wrenched it away and, with quiet bow, restored it to its rightful owner.

"Oh, I say, now, Jerrold, that's downright unhandsome of you!" gasped Sloat. "I'd have been on my way home with it."

"Shut up, you fool!" was the sharp, hissing whisper. "Wait till I go home, if you want to talk about it." And, as quickly as he came, Mr. Jerrold slipped out again upon the piazza.

Of course the story was told with varied comment all over the post. Several officers were injudicious enough to chaff the old subaltern about it, and—he was a little sore-headed the next day, anyway—the usually placid Sloat grew the more indignant at Jerrold. He decided to go and upbraid him; and, as ill luck would have it, they met before noon on the steps of the club-room.

"I want to say to you, Mr. Jerrold, that from an officer of your age to one of mine I think your conduct last night a piece of impertinence."

"I had a perfect right to do what I did," replied Jerrold, coolly. "You were taking a most unwarrantable liberty in trying to carry off that picture."

"How did you know what it was? You had never seen it!"

"There's where you are mistaken, Mr. Sloat" (and Jerrold purposely and exasperatingly refused to recognize the customary *brevet*): "I had seen it,—frequently."

Two officers were standing by, and one of them turned

sharply and faced Jerrold as he spoke. It was his former company commander. Jerrold noted the symptom, and flushed, but set his teeth doggedly.

"Why, Mr. Jerrold! Mrs. Maynard said she never showed that to any one," said Sloat, in much surprise. "You heard her, did you not, Captain Chester?"

"I did, certainly," was the reply.

"All the same, I repeat what I've said," was Jerrold's sullen answer. "I have seen it frequently, and, what's more—" He suddenly stopped.

"Well, what's more?" said Sloat, suggestively.

"Never mind. I don't care to talk of the matter," replied Jerrold, and started to walk away.

But Sloat was angry, nettled, jealous. He had meant to show his intense loyalty and admiration for everything that was his colonel's, and had been snubbed and called a fool by an officer many years, though not so many "files," his junior. He never had liked him, and now there was an air of conscious superiority about Jerrold that fairly exasperated him. He angrily followed and called to him to stop, but Jerrold walked on. Captain Chester stood still and watched them. The little man had almost to run before he overtook the tall one. They were out of earshot when he finally did so. There were a few words on both sides. Then Jerrold shifted his light cane into his left hand, and Chester started forward, half expecting a fracas. To his astonishment, the two officers shook hands and parted.

"Well," said he, as Sloat came back with an angry yet bewildered face, "I'm glad you shook hands. I almost feared a row, and was just going to stop it. So he apologized, did he?"

"No, nothing like it."

"Then what did you mean by shaking hands?"

"That's nothing—never you mind," said Sloat, confusedly. "I haven't forgiven him, by a good deal. The man's conceit is enough to disgust anything—but a woman, I suppose," he finished, ruefully.

"Well, it's none of my business, Sloat, but pardon my saying I don't see what there was to bring about the apparent reconciliation. That hand-shake meant something."

"Oh, well—damn it! we had some words, and he—or I— Well, there's a bet, and we shook hands on it."

"Seems to me that's pretty serious business, Sloat,—a bet following such a talk as you two have had. I hope—"

"Well, captain," interrupted Sloat, "I wouldn't have done it if I hadn't been mad as blazes; but I made it, and must stick to it,—that's all."

"You wouldn't mind telling me what it was, I suppose?"

"I can't; and that ends it."

Captain Chester found food for much thought and specu-lation over this incident. So far as he was concerned, the abrupt remark of Sloat by no means ended it. In his distrust of Jerrold, he too had taken alarm at the very substantial intimacy to which that young man was welcomed at the colonel's quarters. Prior to his marriage old Maynard had not liked him at all, but it was mainly because he had been so negligent of his duties and so determined a beau in city society after his arrival at Sibley. He had, indeed, threatened to have him transferred to a company still on frontier service if he did not reform; but then the rifle-practice season began, and Jerrold was a capital shot and sure to be on the list of competitors for the Department team, so what was the use? He would be ordered in for the rifle-camp anyway, and so the colonel decided to keep him at head-quarters. This was in the summer of the year gone by. Then came the colonel's long leave, his visit to Europe, his meeting with his old friend, now the widow of the lamented Renwick, their delightful winter together in Italy, his courtship, her consent, their marriage and return to America. When Maynard came back to Sibley and the old regiment, he was so jolly and content that every man was welcomed at his house, and it was really a source of pride and pleasure to him that his accomplished wife should find any of his young officers so thoroughly agreeable as she pronounced Mr. Jerrold. Others were soldierly, courteous, well bred, but he had the air of a foreign court about him, she privately informed her lord; and it seems, indeed, that in days gone by Mr. Jerrold's father had spent many years in France and Spain, once as his country's representative near the throne. Though the father died long before the boy was out of his knickerbockers, he had left the impress of his grand manner, and Jerrold, to women of any age, was at once a courtier and a knight. But the colonel never saw how her eyes followed the tall young officer time and again. There were women who soon noted it, and one of them said it was such a yearning, longing look. *Was* Mrs. Maynard really happy? they asked each other. *Did* she really want to see Alice mate with him, the handsome, the dangerous, the selfish fellow they knew him to be? If not, could anything be more imprudent than that they should be thrown together as they were being, day after day? Had Alice wealth of her own? If not, did the mother know that nothing would tempt Howard Jerrold into an alliance with a dowerless daughter? These, and many more, were questions that came up every day. The garrison could talk of little else; and Alice Renwick had been there just three weeks, and was the acknowledged Queen of Hearts at Sibley, when the rifle-competitions began again, and a great array of officers and men from all over the Northwest came to the post by every train, and their canvas tents dotted the broad prairie to the north.

One lovely evening in August, just before the practice began, Colonel Maynard took his wife to drive out and see the camp. Mr. Jerrold and Alice Renwick followed on horse-back. The carriage was surrounded as it halted near the range, and half a score of officers, old and young, were chatting with Mrs. Maynard, while others gathered about the lovely girl who sat there in the saddle. There came marching up from the railway a small squad of soldiers, competitors arriving from the far West. Among them—apparently their senior non-commissioned officer—was a tall cavalry sergeant, superbly built, and with a bronzed and bearded and swarthy face that seemed to tell of years of campaigning over mountain and prairie. They were all men of perfect physique, all in the neat, soldierly fatigue-dress of the regular service, some wearing the spotless white stripes of the infantry, others the less artistic and equally destructible yellow of the cavalry. Their swinging stride, erect carriage, and clear and handsome eyes all spoke of the perfection of health and soldierly development. Curious glances were turned to them as they advanced, and Miss Renwick, catching sight of the party, exclaimed,—

"Oh, who are these? And what a tall soldier that sergeant is!"

"That sergeant, Miss Renwick," said a slow, deliberate voice, "is the man I believe will knock Mr. Jerrold out of the first prize. That is Sergeant McLeod."

As though he heard his name pronounced, the tall cavalryman glanced for the first time at the group, brought his rifle to the carry as if about to salute, and was just stepping upon the roadside, where he came in full view of the occupants of the carriage, when a sudden pallor shot across his face, and he plunged heavily forward and went down like a shot. Sympathetic officers and comrades surrounded the prostrate form in an instant. The colonel himself sprang from his carriage and joined the group; a blanket was quickly brought from a neighboring tent, and the sergeant was borne thither and laid upon a cot. A surgeon felt his pulse and looked inquiringly around:

"Any of you cavalrymen know him well? Has he been affected this way before?"

A young corporal who had been bending anxiously over the sergeant straightened up and saluted:

"I know him well, sir, and have been with him five years. He's only had one sick spell in all that time,—'twas just like this,—and then he told me he'd been sunstruck once."

"This is no case of sunstroke," said the doctor. "It looks more like the heart. How long ago was the attack you speak of?"

"Three years ago last April, sir. I remember it because we'd just got into Fort Raines after a long scout. He'd been the solidest man in the troop all through the cold and storm and snow we had in the mountains, and we were in the reading-room, and he'd picked up a newspaper and was reading while the rest of us were talking and laughing, and, first thing we knew, he was down on the floor, just like he was to-night."

"Hm!" said the surgeon. "Yes. That's plenty, steward. Give him that. Raise his head a little, corporal. Now he'll come round all right."

Driving homeward that night, Colonel Maynard musingly remarked,—

"Did you see that splendid fellow who fainted away?"

"No," answered his wife, "you all gathered about him so quickly and carried him away. I could not even catch a glimpse of him. But he had recovered, had he not?"

"Yes. Still, I was thinking what a singular fact it is that occasionally a man slips through the surgeon's examinations with such a malady as this. Now, here is one of the finest athletes and shots in the whole army, a man who has been through some hard service and stirring fights, has won a tip-top name for himself and was on the highroad to a commission, and yet this will block him effectually."

"Why, what is the trouble?"

"Some affection of the heart. Why! Halloo! Stop, driver! Orderly, jump down and run back there. Mrs. Maynard has dropped her fan.—What was it, dear?" he asked, anxiously. "You started; and you are white, and trembling."

"I—I don't know, colonel. Let us go home. It will be over in a minute. Where are Alice and Mr. Jerrold? Call them, please. She must not be out riding after dark."

But they were not in sight; and it was considerably after dark when they reached the fort. Mr. Jerrold explained that his horse had picked up a stone and he had had to walk him all the way.

IV

There was no sleep for Captain Chester the rest of the night. He went home, threw off his sword-belt, and seated himself in a big easy-chair before his fireplace, deep in thought. Once or twice he arose and paced restlessly up and down the room, as he had done in his excited talk with Rollins some few hours before. Then he was simply angry and argumentative,—or declamatory. Now he had settled down into a very different frame of mind. He seemed awed,—stunned,—crushed. He had all the bearing and mien of one who, having defiantly predicted a calamity, was thunderstruck by the verification of his prophecy. In all his determined arraignment of Mr. Jerrold, in all the harsh things he had said and thought of him, he had never imagined any such depth of scoundrelism as the revelations of the night foreshadowed. Chester differed from many of his brotherhood: there was no room for rejoicing in his heart that the worst he had ever said of Jerrold was unequal to the apparent truth. He took no comfort to his soul that those who called him cynical, crabbed, unjust, even malicious, would now be compelled to admit he was right in his estimate. Like the best of us, Chester could not ordinarily say "*Vade retro*" to the temptation to think, if not to say, "Didn't I tell you so?" when in every-day affairs his oft-disputed views were proved well founded. But in the face of such a catastrophe as now appeared engulfing the fair fame of his regiment and the honor of those whom his colonel held dear, Chester could feel only dismay and grief. What was his duty in the light of the discoveries he had made? To the best of his belief, he was the only man in the garrison who had evidence of Jerrold's absence from his own quarters and of the presence of *some one* at *her* window. He had taken prompt measures to prevent its being suspected by others. He purposely sent his guards to search along the cliff in the opposite direction while he went to Jerrold's room and thence back to remove the tell-tale ladder. Should he tell *any* one until he had confronted Jerrold with the evidences of his guilt, and, wringing from him his resignation, send him far from the post before handing it in? Time and again he wished Frank Armitage were here. The youngest captain in the regiment, Armitage had been for years its adjutant and deep in the confidence of Colonel Maynard. He was a thorough soldier, a strong, self-reliant, courageous man, and one for whom Chester had ever felt a warm esteem. Armitage was on leave of absence, however,—had been away some time on account of family matters, and would not return, it was known, until he had effected the removal of his mother and sister to the new home he had purchased for them in the distant East. It was to his company that Jerrold had been promoted, and there was friction from the very week that the handsome subaltern joined.

Armitage had long before "taken his measure," and was in no wise pleased that so lukewarm a soldier should have come to him as senior subaltern. They had a very plain talk, for Armitage was straightforward as a dart, and then, as Jerrold showed occasional lapses, the captain shut down on some of his most cherished privileges, and, to the indignation of society, the failure of Mr. Jerrold to appear at one or two gatherings where he was confidently expected was speedily laid at his captain's door. The recent death of his father kept Armitage from appearing in public, and, as neither he nor the major (who commanded the regiment while Maynard was abroad) vouchsafed the faintest explanation, society was allowed to form its own conclusions, and *did*,—to the effect that Mr. Jerrold was a wronged and persecuted man. It was just as the Maynards arrived at Sibley that Armitage departed on his leave, and, to his unspeakable bliss, Mr. Jerrold succeeded to the command of his company. This fact, coupled with the charming relations which were straightway established with the colonel's family, placed him in a position of independence and gave him opportunities he had never known before. It was speedily evident that he was neglecting his military duties,—that Company B was running down much faster than Armitage had built it up,— and yet no man felt like speaking of it to the colonel, who saw it only occasionally on dress-parade. Chester had just about determined to write to Armitage himself and suggest his speedy return, when this eventful night arrived. Now he fully made up his mind that it must be done at once, and had seated himself at his desk, when the roar of the sunrise gun and the blare of the bugles warned him that reveille had come and he must again go to his guard. Before he returned to his quarters another complication, even more embarrassing, had arisen, and the letter to Armitage was postponed.

He had received the "present" of his guard and verified the presence of all his prisoners, when he saw Major Sloat still standing out in the middle of the parade, where the adjutant usually received the reports of the roll-calls. Several company officers, having made their reports, were scurrying back to quarters for another snooze before breakfast-time or to get their cup of coffee before going out to the range. Chester strolled over towards him.

"What's the matter, Sloat?"

"Nothing much. The colonel told me to receive the reveille

reports for Hoyt this week. He's on general court-martial."

"Yes, I know all that. I mean, what are you waiting for?"

"Mr. Jerrold again. There's no report from his company."

"Have you sent to wake him?"

"No; I'll go myself, and do it thoroughly, too." And the little major turned sharply away and walked direct to the low range of bachelor quarters, dove under the piazza, and into the green door-way.

Hardly knowing how to explain his action, Chester quickly followed, and in less than a minute was standing in the self-same parlor which, by the light of a flickering match, he had searched two hours before. Here he halted and listened, while Sloat pushed on into the bedroom and was heard vehemently apostrophizing some sleeper:

"Does the government pay you for this sort of thing, I want to know? Get up, Jerrold! This is the second time you've cut reveille in ten days. Get up, I say!" And the major was vigorously shaking at something, for the bed creaked and groaned.

"Wake up! I say, I'm blowed if I'm going to get up here day after day and have you sleeping. Wake, Nicodemus! Wake, you snoozing, snoring, open-mouthed masher. Come, now; I mean it."

A drowsy, disgusted yawn and stretch finally rewarded his efforts. Mr. Jerrold at last opened his eyes, rolled over, yawned sulkily again, and tried to evade his persecutor, but to no purpose. Like a little terrier, Sloat hung on to him and worried and shook.

"Oh, don't! damn it, don't!" growled the victim. "What do you want, anyway? Has that infernal reveille gone?"

"Yes, and you're absent again, and no report from B Company. By the holy poker, if you don't turn out and get it and report to me on the parade I'll spot the whole gang absent, and then no *matinee* for you to-day, my buck. Come, out with you! I mean it. Hall says you and he have an engagement in town; and 'pon my soul I'll bust it if you don't come out."

And so, growling and complaining, and yet half laughing, Adonis rolled from his couch and began to get into his clothes. Chester's blood ran cold, then boiled. Think of a man who could laugh like that,—and remember! *When*, how, had he returned to the house? Listen!

"Confound you, Sloat, *I* wouldn't rout *you* out in this shabby way. Why couldn't you let a man sleep? I'm tired half to death."

"What have you done to tire you? Slept all yesterday afternoon, and danced perhaps a dozen times at the doctor's last night. You've had more sleep than I've had, begad! You took Miss Renwick home before 'twas over, and mean it was of you, too, with all the fellows that wanted to dance with her."

"That wasn't my fault: Mrs. Maynard made her promise to be home at twelve. You old cackler, that's what sticks in your crop yet. You are persecuting me because they like me so much better than they do you," he went on, laughingly now. "Come, now, Sloat, confess, it is all because you're jealous. You couldn't have that picture, and I could."

Chester fairly started. He had urgent need to see this young gallant,—he was staying for that purpose,—but should he listen to further talk like this? Too late to move, for Sloat's answer came like a shot:

"I bet you you *never* could!"

"But didn't I tell you I had?—a week ago?"

"Ay, but I didn't believe it. You couldn't show it!"

"Pshaw, man! Look here. Stop, though! Remember, *on your honor*, you never tell."

"On my honor, of course."

"Well, there!"

A drawer was opened. Chester heard a gulp of dismay, of genuine astonishment and conviction mixed, as Sloat muttered some half-articulate words and then came into the front room. Jerrold followed, caught sight of Chester, and stopped short, with sudden and angry change of color.

"I did not know *you* were here," he said.

"It was to find where *you* were that I came," was the quiet answer.

There was a moment's silence. Sloat turned and looked at the two men in utter surprise. Up to this time he had considered Jerrold's absence from reveille as a mere dereliction of duty which was ascribable to the laziness and indifference of the young officer. So far as lay in his power, he meant to make him attend more strictly to business, and had therefore come to his quarters and stirred him up. But there was no thought of any serious trouble in his mind. His talk had all been roughly good-humored until—until that bet was mentioned, and then it became earnest. Now, as he glanced from one man to the other, he saw in an instant that something new— something of unusual gravity—was impending. Chester, buttoned to the throat in his dark uniform, accurately gloved and belted, with pale, set, almost haggard face, was standing by the centre-table under the drop-light. Jerrold, only half dressed, his feet thrust into slippers, his fingers nervously working at the studs of his dainty white shirt, had stopped short at his bedroom door, and, with features that grew paler every second and a dark scowl on his brow, was glowering at Chester.

"Since when has it been the duty of the officer of the day to come around and hunt up officers who don't happen to be out at reveille?" he asked.

"It is not your absence from reveille I want explained, Mr. Jerrold," was the cold and deliberate answer. "I wanted you at 3.30 this morning, and you were not and had not been here."

An unmistakable start and shock; a quick, nervous, hunted glance around the room, so cold and pallid in the early light of the August morning; a clutch of Jerrold's slim brown hand at the bared throat. But he rallied gamely, strode a step forward, and looked his superior full in the face. Sloat marked the effort with which he cleared away the huskiness that seemed to clog his larynx, but admired the spunk with which the young officer returned the senior's shot:

"What is your authority here, I would like to know? What business has the officer of the day to want me or any other man not on guard? Captain Chester, you seem to forget that I am no longer your second lieutenant, and that I am a company commander like yourself. Do you come by Colonel Maynard's order to search my quarters and question me? If so, say so at once; if not, get out." And Jerrold's face was growing black with wrath, and his big lustrous eyes were wide awake now and fairly snapping.

Chester leaned upon the table and deliberated a moment. He stood there coldly, distrustfully eying the excited lieutenant, then turned to Sloat:

"I will be responsible for the roll-call of Company B this morning, Sloat. I have a matter of grave importance to bring up to this—this gentleman, and it is of a private nature. Will you let me see him alone?"

"Sloat," said Jerrold, "don't go yet. I want you to stay. These are my quarters, and I recognize your right to come here in search of me, since I was not at reveille; but I want a witness here to bear me out. I'm too amazed yet—too confounded by this intrusion of Captain Chester's to grasp the situation. I never heard of such a thing as this. Explain it, if you can."

"Mr. Jerrold, what I have to ask or say to you concerns you alone. It is *not* an official matter. It is as man to man I want to see you, alone and at once. *Now* will you let Major Sloat retire?"

Silence for a moment. The angry flush on Jerrold's face was dying away, and in its place an ashen pallor was spreading from throat to brow; his lips were twitching ominously. Sloat looked in consternation at the sudden change.

"Shall I go?" he finally asked.

Jerrold looked long, fixedly, searchingly in the set face of the officer of the day, breathing hard and heavily. What he saw there Sloat could not imagine. At last his hand dropped by his side; he made a little motion with it, a slight wave towards the door, and again dropped it nervously. His lips seemed to frame the word "Go," but he never glanced at the man whom a moment before he so masterfully bade to stay; and Sloat, sorely puzzled, left the room.

Not until his footsteps had died out of hearing did Chester speak:

"How soon can you leave the post?"

"I don't understand you."

"How soon can you pack up what you need to take and—get away?"

"Get away where? What on earth do you mean?"

"You *must* know what I mean! You *must* know that after last night's work you quit the service at once and forever."

"I don't know anything of the kind; and I defy you to prove the faintest thing." But Jerrold's fingers were twitching, and his eyes had lost their light.

"Do you suppose I did not recognize you?" asked Chester.

"When?—where?" gulped Jerrold.

"When I seized you and you struck me!"

"I never struck you. I don't know what you mean."

"My God, man, let us end this useless fencing. The evidence I have of your last night's scoundrelism would break the strongest record. For the regiment's sake,—for the colonel's sake,—let us have no public scandal. It's awful enough as the thing stands. Write your resignation, give it to me, and leave,—before breakfast if you can."

"I've done nothing to resign for. You know perfectly well I haven't."

"Do you mean that such a crime—that a woman's ruin and disgrace—isn't enough to drive you from the service?" asked Chester, tingling in every nerve and longing to clinch the shapely, swelling throat in his clutching fingers. "God of heaven, Jerrold! are you dead to all sense of decency?"

"Captain Chester, I won't be bullied this way. I may not be immaculate, but no man on earth shall talk to me like this! I deny your insinuations. I've done nothing to warrant your words, even if—if you did come sneaking around here last night and find me absent. You can't prove a thing. You—"

"What! When I saw you,—almost caught you! By heaven! I wish the sentry had killed you then and there. I never dreamed of such hardihood."

"You've done nothing but dream. By Jove, I believe you're sleepwalking yet. What on earth do you mean by catching and killing me? 'Pon my soul I reckon you're crazy, Captain Chester." And color was gradually coming back again to Jerrold's face, and confidence to his tone.

"Enough of this, Mr. Jerrold. Knowing what you and I both know, do you refuse to hand me your resignation?"

"Of course I do."

"Do you mean to deny to me where I saw you last night?"

"I deny your right to question me. I deny anything,—

everything. I believe you simply thought you had a clue and could make me tell. Suppose I *was* out last night. I don't believe you know the faintest thing about it."

"Do you want me to report the whole thing to the colonel?"

"Of course I don't. Naturally, I want him to know nothing about my being out of quarters; and it's a thing that no officer would think of reporting another for. You'll only win the contempt of every gentleman in the regiment if you do it. What good will it do you?—Keep me from going to town for a few days, I suppose. What earthly business is it of yours, anyway?"

"Jerrold, I can stand this no longer. I ought to shoot you in your tracks, I believe. You've brought ruin and misery to the home of my warmest friend, and dishonor to the whole service, and you talk of two or three days' stoppage from going to town. If I can't bring you to your senses, by God! the colonel shall." And he wheeled and left the room.

For a moment Jerrold stood stunned and silent. It was useless to attempt reply. The captain was far down the walk when he sprang to the door to call him again. Then, hurrying back to the bedroom, he hastily dressed, muttering angrily and anxiously to himself as he did so. He was thinking deeply, too, and every movement betrayed nervousness and trouble. Returning to the front door, he gazed out upon the parade, then took his forage-cap and walked rapidly down towards the adjutant's office. The orderly bugler was tilted up in a chair, leaning half asleep against the whitewashed front, but his was a weasel nap, for he sprang up and saluted as the young officer approached.

"Where did Major Sloat go, orderly?" was the hurried question.

"Over towards the stables, sir. Him and Captain Chester was here together, and they're just gone."

"Run over to the quarters of B Company and tell Merrick I want him right away. Tell him to come to my quarters." And thither Mr. Jerrold returned, seated himself at his desk, wrote several lines of a note, tore it into fragments, began again, wrote another which seemed not entirely satisfactory, and was in the midst of a third when there came a quick step and a knock at the door. Opening the shutters, he glanced out of the window. A gust of wind sent some of the papers whirling and flying, and the bedroom door banged shut, but not before some few half-sheets of paper had fluttered out upon the parade, where other little flurries of the morning breeze sent them sailing over towards the colonel's quarters. Anxious only for the coming of Merrick and no one else, Mr. Jerrold no sooner saw who was at the front door than he closed the shutters, called, "Come in!" and a short, squat, wiry little man, dressed in the fatigue-uniform of the infantry, stood at the door-way to the hall.

"Come in here, Merrick," said the lieutenant, and Merrick came.

"How much is it you owe me now?—thirty-odd dollars, I think?"

"I believe it is, lieutenant," answered the man, with shifting eyes and general uneasiness of mien.

"You are not ready to pay it, I suppose; and you got it from me when we left Fort Raines, to help you out of that scrape there."

The soldier looked down and made no answer.

"Merrick, I want a note taken to town at once. I want *you* to take it and get it to its address before eight o'clock. I want you to say no word to a soul. Here's ten dollars. Hire old Murphy's horse across the river and *go*. If you are put in the guard-house when you get back, don't say a word; if you are tried by garrison court for crossing the bridge or absence without leave, plead guilty, make no defence, and I'll pay you double your fine and let you off the thirty dollars. But if you fail me, or tell a soul of your errand, I'll write to—you know who, at Raines. Do you understand, and agree?"

"I do. Yessir."

"Go and get ready, and be here in ten minutes."

Meantime, Captain Chester had followed Sloat to the adjutant's office. He was boiling over with indignation which he hardly knew how to control. He found the gray-moustached subaltern tramping in great perplexity up and down the room, and the instant he entered was greeted with the inquiry,—

"What's gone wrong? What's Jerrold been doing?"

"Don't ask me any questions, Sloat, but answer. It is a matter of honor. *What* was your bet with Jerrold?"

"I oughtn't to tell that, Chester. Surely it cannot be a matter mixed up with this."

"I can't explain, Sloat. What I ask is unavoidable. Tell me about that bet."

"Why, he was so superior and airy, you know, and was trying to make me feel that he was so much more intimate with them all at the colonel's, and that he could have that picture for the mere asking; and I got mad, and bet him he *never* could."

"Was that the day you shook hands on it?"

"Yes."

"And that was her picture—*the* picture, then—he showed you this morning."

"Chester, you heard the conversation: you were there: you know that I'm on honor not to tell."

"Yes, I know. That's quite enough."

V

Before seven o'clock that same morning Captain Chester had come to the conclusion that only one course was left open for him. After the brief talk with Sloat at the office he had increased the perplexity and distress of that easily-muddled soldier by requesting his company in a brief visit to the stables and corrals. A "square" and reliable old veteran was the quartermaster sergeant who had charge of those establishments; Chester had known him for years, and his fidelity and honesty were matters the officers of his former regiment could not too highly commend. When Sergeant Parks made an official statement there was no shaking its solidity. He slept in a little box of a house close by the entrance to the main stable, in which were kept the private horses of several of the officers, and among them Mr. Jerrold's; and it was his boast that, day or night, no horse left that stable without his knowledge. The old man was superintending the morning labors of the stable-hands, and looked up in surprise at so early a visit from the officer of the day.

"Were you here all last night, sergeant?" was Chester's abrupt question.

"Certainly, sir, and up until one o'clock or more."

"Were any horses out during the night,—any officers' horses, I mean?"

"No, sir, not one."

"I thought possibly some officers might have driven or ridden to town."

"No, sir. The only horses that crossed this threshold going out last night were Mr. Sutton's team from town. They were put up here until near one o'clock, and then the doctor sent over for them. I locked up right after that, and can swear nothing else went out."

Chester entered the stable and looked curiously around. Presently his eye lighted on a tall, rangy bay horse that was being groomed in a wide stall near the door-way.

"That's Mr. Jerrold's Roderick, isn't it?"

"Yes, sir. He's fresh as a daisy, too,—hasn't been out for three days,—and Mr. Jerrold's going to drive the dog-cart this morning."

Chester turned away.

"Sloat," said he, as they left the stable, "if Mr. Jerrold was away from the post last night,—and you heard me say he was out of his quarters,—could he have gone any way except afoot, after what you heard Parks say?"

"Gone in the Suttons' outfit, I suppose," was Sloat's cautious answer.

"In which event he would have been seen by the sentry at the bridge, would he not?"

"Ought to have been, certainly."

"Then we'll go back to the guard-house." And, wonderingly and uncomfortably, Sloat followed. He had long since begun to wish he had held his peace and said nothing about the confounded roll-call. He hated rows of any kind. He didn't like Jerrold, but he would have crawled *ventre a terre* across the wide parade sooner than see a scandal in the regiment he loved; and it was becoming apparent to his sluggish faculties that it was no mere matter of absence from quarters that was involving Jerrold. Chester was all aflame over that picture-business, he remembered, and the whole drift of his present investigation was to prove that Jerrold was *not* absent from the post, but absent only from his quarters. If so, where had he spent his time until nearly four? Sloat's heart was heavy with vague apprehension. He knew that Jerrold had borne Alice Renwick away from the party at an unusually early hour for such things to break up. He knew that he and others had protested against such desertion, but she declared it could not be helped. He remembered another thing,—a matter that he thought of at the time, only from another point of view. It now seemed to have significance bearing on this very matter; for Chester suddenly asked,—

"Wasn't it rather odd that Miss Beaubien was not here at the dance? She has never missed one, seems to me, since Jerrold began spooning with her last year."

"Why, she *was* here."

"She was? Are you sure? Rollins never spoke of it; and we had been talking of her. I inferred from what he said that she was not there at all. And I saw her drive homeward with her mother right after parade: so it didn't occur to me that she could have come out again, all that distance, in time for the dance. Singular! Why shouldn't Rollins have told me?"

Sloat grinned: a dreary sort of smile it was, too. "You go into society so seldom you don't see these things. I've more than half suspected Rollins of being quite ready to admire Miss Beaubien himself; and since Jerrold dropped her he has had plenty of opportunity."

"Great guns! I never thought of it! If I'd known she was to be there I'd have gone myself last night. How did she behave to Miss Renwick?"

"Why, sweet and smiling, and chipper as you please. If anything, I think Miss Renwick was cold and distant to her. I couldn't make it out at all."

"And did Jerrold dance with her?"

"Once, I think, and they had a talk out on the piazza,—just a minute. I happened to be at the door, and couldn't help seeing it; and what got me was this: Mr. Hall came out with Miss Renwick on his arm; they were chatting and laughing as they passed me, but the moment she caught sight of Jerrold and Miss Beaubien she stopped, and said, 'I think I won't stay out here; it's too chilly,' or something like it, and went right in; and then Jerrold dropped Miss Beaubien and went after her. He just handed the young lady over to me, saying he was engaged for next dance, and skipped."

"How did she like that? Wasn't she furious?"

"No. That's another thing that got me. She smiled after him, all sweetness, and—well, she *did* say, 'I count upon you,— you'll be there,' and he nodded. Oh, she was bright as a button after that."

"What did she mean?—be 'where,' do you suppose? Sloat, this all means more to me, and to us all, than I can explain."

"I don't know. I can't imagine."

"Was it to see her again that night?"

"I don't know at all. If it was, he fooled her, for he never went near her again. Rollins put her in the carriage."

"Whose? Did she come out with the Suttons?"

"Why, certainly. I thought you knew that."

"And neither old Madame Beaubien nor Mrs. Sutton with them? What was the old squaw thinking of?"

By this time they had neared the guard-house, where several of the men were seated awaiting the call for the next relief. All arose at the shout of the sentry on Number One, turning out the guard for the officer of the day. Chester made hurried and impatient acknowledgment of the salute, and called to the sergeant to send him the sentry who was at the bridge at one o'clock. It turned out to be a young soldier who had enlisted at the post only six months before and was already known as one of the most intelligent and promising candidates for a corporalship in the garrison.

"Were you on duty at the bridge at one o'clock, Carey?" asked the captain.

"I was, sir. My relief went on at 11.45 and came off at 1.45."

"What persons passed your post during that time?"

"There was a squad or two of men coming back from town on pass. I halted them, sir, and Corporal Murray came down and passed them in."

"I don't mean coming from town. Who went the other way?"

"Only one carriage, sir,—Mr. Sutton's."

"Could you see who were in it?"

"Certainly, sir: it was right under the lamp-post this end of the bridge that I stood when I challenged. Lieutenant Rollins answered for them and passed them out. He was sitting beside Mr. Sutton as they drove up, then jumped out and gave me the countersign and bade them good-night right there."

"Rollins again," thought Chester. "Why did he keep this from me?"

"Who were in the carriage?" he asked.

"Mr. Sutton, sir, on the front seat, driving, and two young ladies on the back seat."

"Nobody else?"

"Not a soul, sir. I could see in it plain as day. One lady was Miss Sutton, and the other Miss Beaubien. I know I was surprised at seeing the latter, because she drove home in her own carriage last evening right after parade. I was on post there at that hour too, sir. The second relief is on from 5.45 to 7.45."

"That will do, Carey. I see your relief is forming now."

As the officers walked away and Sloat silently plodded along beside his dark-browed senior, the latter turned to him:

"I should say that there was no way in which Mr. Jerrold

could have gone townwards last night. Should not you?"

"He might have crossed the bridge while the third relief was on, and got a horse at the other side."

"He didn't do that, Sloat. I had already questioned the sentry on that relief. It was the third that I inspected and visited this morning."

"Well, how do you know he wanted to go to town? Why couldn't he have gone up the river, or out to the range? Perhaps there was a little game of 'draw' out at camp."

"There was no light in camp, much less a little game of draw, after eleven o'clock. You know well enough that there is nothing of that kind going on with Gaines in command. That isn't Jerrold's game, even if those fellows *were* bent on ruining their eyesight and nerve and spoiling the chance of getting the men on the division and army teams. I wish it *were* his game, instead of what it is!"

"Still, Chester, he may have been out in the country somewhere. You seem bent on the conviction he was up to mischief here, around this post. I won't ask you what you mean; but there's more than one way of getting to town if a man wants to very bad."

"How? Of course he can take a skiff and row down the river; but he'd never be back in time for reveille. There goes six o'clock, and I must get home and shave and think this over. Keep your own counsel, no matter who asks you. If you hear any questions or talk about shooting last night, you know nothing, heard nothing, and saw nothing."

"Shooting last night!" exclaimed Sloat, all agog with eagerness and excitement now. "Where was it? Who was it?"

But Chester turned a deaf ear upon him, and walked away. He wanted to see Rollins, and went straight home.

"Why didn't you tell me Miss Beaubien was out here last night?" was the question he asked as soon as he had entered the room where, all aglow from his cold bath, the youngster was dressing for breakfast. He colored vividly, then laughed.

"Well, you never gave me much chance to say anything, did you? You talked all the time, as I remember, and suddenly vanished and slammed the door. I would have told you had you asked me." But all the same it was evident for the first time that here was a subject Rollins was shy of mentioning.

"Did you go down and see them across sentry post?"

"Certainly. Jerrold asked me to. He said he had to take Miss Renwick home, and was too tired to come back,—was going to turn in. I was glad to do anything to be civil to the Suttons."

"Why, I'd like to know? They have never invited you to the house or shown you any attention whatever. You are not their style at all, Rollins, and I'm glad of it. It wasn't for their sake you stayed there until one o'clock instead of being here in bed. I wish—" and he looked wistfully, earnestly, at his favorite now, "I wish I could think it wasn't for the sake of Miss Beaubien's black eyes and aboriginal beauty."

"Look here, captain," said Rollins, with another rush of color to his face; "you don't seem to fancy Miss Beaubien, and— she's a friend of mine, and one I don't like to hear slightingly spoken of. You said a good deal last night that—well, wasn't pleasant to hear."

"I know it, Rollins. I beg your pardon. I didn't know then that you were more than slightly acquainted with her. I'm an old bat, and go out very little, but some things are pretty clear to my eyes, and—don't you be falling in love with Nina Beaubien. That is no match for you."

"I'm sure you never had a word to say against her father. The old colonel was a perfect type of the French gentleman, from all I hear."

"Yes, and her mother is as perfect a type of a Chippewa squaw, if she is only a half-breed and claims to be only a sixteenth. Rollins, there's Indian blood enough in Nina Beaubien's little finger to make me afraid of her. She is strong as death in love or hate, and you must have seen how she hung on Jerrold's every word all last winter. You must know she is not the girl to be lightly dropped now."

"She told me only a day or two ago they were the best of friends and had never been anything else," said Rollins, hotly.

"Has it gone that far, my boy? I had not thought it so bad, by any means. It's no use talking with a man who has lost his heart: his reason goes with it." And Chester turned away.

"You don't know anything about it," was all poor Rollins could think of as a suitable thing to shout after him; and it made no more impression than it deserved.

As has been said, Captain Chester had decided before seven o'clock that but one course lay open to him in the matter as now developed. Had Armitage been there he would have had an adviser, but there was no other man whose counsel he eared to seek. Old Captain Gray was as bitter against Jerrold as Chester himself, and with even better reason, for he knew well the cause of his little daughter's listless manner and tearful eyes. She had been all radiance and joy at the idea of coming to Sibley and being near the great cities, but not one happy look had he seen in her sweet and wistful face since the day of her arrival. Wilton, too, was another captain who disliked Jerrold; and Chester's rugged sense of fair play told him that it was not among the enemies of the young officer that he should now seek advice, but that if he had a friend among the older and wiser heads in the regiment it was due to him that that older and wiser head be given a chance to think a little for Jerrold's sake. And there was not one among the seniors whom he could call upon. As he ran over their names, Chester for the first time realized that his ex-subaltern had not a friend among the captains and senior officers now on duty at the fort. His indifference to duties, his airy foppishness, his conceit and self-sufficiency, had all served to create a feeling against him; and this had been intensified by his conduct since coming to Sibley. The youngsters still kept up jovial relations with and professed to like him, but among the seniors there were many men who had only a nod for him on meeting. Wilton had epitomized the situation by saying he "had no use for a masher," and poor old Gray had one day scowlingly referred to him as "the professional beauty."

In view of all this feeling, Chester would gladly have found some man to counsel further delay; but there was none. He felt that he must inform the colonel at once of the fact that Mr. Jerrold was absent from his quarters at the time of the firing, of his belief that it was Jerrold who struck him and sped past the sentry in the dark, and of his conviction that the sooner the young officer was called to account for his strange conduct the better. As to the episodes of the ladder, the lights, and the form at the dormer-window, he meant, for the present at least, to lock them in his heart.

But he forgot that others too must have heard those shots, and that others too would be making inquiries.

VI

A lovely morning it was that beamed on Sibley and the broad and beautiful valley of the Cloudwater when once the sun got fairly above the moist horizon. Mist and vapor and heavy cloud all seemed swallowed up in the gathering, glowing warmth, as though the King of Day had risen athirst and drained the welcoming cup of nature. It must have rained at least a little during the darkness of the night, for dew there could have been none with skies so heavily overcast, and yet the short smooth turf on the parade, the leaves upon the little shade-trees around the quadrangle, and all the beautiful vines here on the trellis-work of the colonel's veranda, shone and sparkled in the radiant light. The roses in the little garden, and the old-fashioned morning-glory vines over at the east side, were all a-glitter in the flooding sunshine when the bugler came out from a glance at the clock in the adjutant's office and sounded "sick-call" to the indifferent ear of the garrison. Once each day, at 7.30 a.m., the doctor trudged across to the hospital and looked over the half-dozen "hopelessly healthy" but would-be invalids who wanted to get off guard duty or a morning at the range. Thanks to the searching examination to which every soldier must be subjected before he can enter the service of Uncle Sam, and to the disciplined order of the lives of the men at Sibley, maladies of any serious nature were almost unknown. It was a gloriously healthy post, as everybody admitted, and, to judge from the specimen of young-womanhood that came singing, "blithe and low," out among the roses this same joyous morning, exuberant physical well-being was not restricted to the men.

A fairer picture never did dark beauty present than Alice Renwick, as she bent among the bushes or reached high among the vines in search of her favorite flowers. Tall, slender, willowy, yet with exquisitely-rounded form; slim, dainty little hands and feet; graceful arms and wrists all revealed in the flowing sleeves of her snowy, web-like gown, fitting her and displaying her sinuous grace of form as gowns so seldom do to-day. And then her face!—a glorious picture of rich, ripe, tropical beauty, with its great, soulful, sunlit eyes, heavily shaded though they were with those wondrous lashes; beautiful, too, in contour as was the lithe body, and beautiful in every feature, even to the rare and dewy curve of her red lips, half opened as she sang. She was smiling to herself, as she crooned her soft, murmuring melody, and every little while the great dark eyes glanced over towards the shaded doors of Bachelors' Row. There was no one up to watch and tell: why should she not look thither, and even stand one moment peering under the veranda at a darkened window half-way down the row, as though impatient at the non-appearance of some familiar signal? How came the laggard late? How slept the knight while here his lady stood impatient? She twined the leaves and roses in a fragrant knot, ran lightly within and laid them on the snowy cloth beside the colonel's seat at table, came forth and plucked some more and fastened them, blushing, blissful, in the lace-fringed opening of her gown, through which, soft and creamy, shone the perfect neck.

"Daisy, tell my fortune, pray:
He loves me not,—he loves me,"

she blithely sang, then, hurrying to the gate, shaded her eyes with the shapely hand and gazed intently. 'Twas nearing eight,—nearing breakfast-time. But some one was coming. Horrid! Captain Chester, of all men! Coming, of course, to see papa, and papa not yet down, and mamma had a headache and had decided not to come down at all, she would breakfast in her room. What girl on earth when looking and longing and waiting for the coming of a graceful youth of twenty-six would be anything but dismayed at the substitution therefor of a bulky, heavy-hearted captain of forty-six, no matter if he were still unmarried? And yet her smile was sweet and cordial.

"Why, good-morning, Captain Chester. I'm so glad to see you this bright day. Do come in and let me give you a rose. Papa will soon be down." And she opened the gate and held forth one long, slim hand. He took it slowly, as though in a dream, raising his forage-cap at the same time, yet making no reply. He was looking at her far more closely than he imagined. How fresh, how radiant, how fair and gracious and winning! Every item of her attire was so pure and white and spotless; every fold and curve of her gown seemed charged with subtile, delicate fragrance, as faint and sweet as the shy and modest wood-violet's. She noted his silence and his haggard eyes. She noted the intent gaze, and the color mounted straightway to her forehead.

"And have you no word of greeting for me?" she blithely laughed, striving to break through the awkwardness of his reserve, "or are you worn out with your night watch as officer of the day?"

He fairly started. Had she seen him, then? Did she know it was he who stood beneath her window, he who leaped in chase of that scoundrel, he who stole away with that heavy tell-tale ladder? and, knowing all this, could she stand there smiling in his face, the incarnation of maiden innocence and beauty? Impossible! Yet what could she mean?

"How did you know I had so long a vigil?" he asked, and the cold, strained tone, the half-averted eyes, the pallor of his face, all struck her at once. Instantly her manner changed:

"Oh, forgive me, captain. I see you are all worn out; and I'm keeping you here at the gate. Come to the piazza and sit down. I'll tell papa you are here, for I know you want to see him." And she tripped lightly away before he could reply, and rustled up the stairs. He could hear her light tap at the colonel's door, and her soft, clear, flute-like voice: "Papa, Captain Chester is here to see you."

Papa indeed! She spoke to him and of him as though he were her own. He treated her as though she were his flesh and blood,—as though he loved her devotedly. Even before she came had not they been prepared for this? Did not Mrs. Maynard tell them that Alice had become enthusiastically devoted to her step-father and considered him the most knightly and chivalric hero she had ever seen? He could hear the colonel's hearty and loving tone in reply, and then she came fluttering down again:

"Papa will be with you in five minutes, captain. But won't you let me give you some coffee? It's all ready, and you look so tired,—even ill."

"I have had a bad night," he answered, "but I'm growing old, and cannot stand sleeplessness as you young people seem to."

Was she faltering? He watched her eagerly, narrowly, almost wonderingly. Not a trace of confusion, not a sign of fear; and yet had he not *seen* her, and that other figure?

"I wish you could sleep as I do," was the prompt reply. "I was in the land of dreams ten minutes after my head touched the pillow, and mamma made me come home early last night because of our journey to-day. You know we are going down to visit Aunt Grace, Colonel Maynard's sister, at Lake Sablon, and mamma wanted me to be looking my freshest and best," she said, "and I never heard a thing till reveille."

His eyes, sad, penetrating, doubting,—yet self-doubting, too,—searched her very soul. Unflinchingly the dark orbs looked into his,—even pityingly; for she quickly spoke again:

"Captain, *do* come into the breakfast-room and have some coffee. You have not breakfasted, I'm sure."

He raised his hand as though to repel her offer,—even to put her aside. He *must* understand her. He *could* not be hood-winked in this way.

"Pardon me, Miss Renwick, but did you hear nothing strange last night or early this morning? Were you not disturbed at all?"

"I? No, indeed!" True, her face had changed now, but there was no fear in her eyes. It was a look of apprehension, perhaps, of concern and curiosity mingled, for his tone betrayed that something had happened which caused him agitation.

"And you heard no shots fired?"

"Shots! No! Oh, Captain Chester! what does it mean? *Who* was shot? Tell me!"

And now, with paling face and wild apprehension in her

eyes, she turned and gazed beyond him, past the vines and the shady veranda, across the sunshine of the parade and under the old piazza, searching that still closed and darkened window.

"Who?" she implored, her hands clasping nervously, her eyes returning eagerly to his face.

"It was not Mr. Jerrold," he answered, coldly. "He is unhurt, so far as shot is concerned."

"Then how is he hurt? Is he hurt at all?" she persisted; and then as she met his gaze her eyes fell, and the burning blush of maiden shame surged up to her forehead. She sank upon a seat and covered her face with her hands.

"I thought of Mr. Jerrold, naturally. He said he would be over early this morning," was all she could find to say.

"I have seen him, and presume he will come. To all appearances, he is the last man to suffer from last night's affair," he went on, relentlessly,—almost brutally,—but she never winced. "It is odd you did not hear the shots. I thought yours was the northwest room,—this one?" he indicated, pointing overhead.

"So it is, and I slept there all last night and heard nothing,—not a thing. *Do* tell me what the trouble was."

Then what was there for him to say? The colonel's footsteps were heard upon the stair, and the colonel, with extended hand and beaming face and cheery welcome, came forth from the open door-way:

"Welcome, Chester! I'm glad you've come just in time for breakfast. Mrs. Maynard won't be down. She slept badly last night, and is sleeping now. What was the firing last night? I did not hear it at the time, but the orderly and old Maria the cook were discussing it as I was shaving."

"It is that I came to see you about, colonel. I am the man to hold responsible."

"No prisoners got away, I hope?"

"No, sir. Nothing, I fear, that would seem to justify my action. I ordered Number Five to fire."

"Why, what on earth could have happened around there,— almost back of us?" said the colonel, in surprise.

"I do not know what had happened, or what was going to happen." And Chester paused a moment, and glanced towards the door through which Miss Renwick had retired as soon as the colonel arrived. The old soldier seemed to understand the glance. "*She* would not listen," he said, proudly.

"I know," explained Chester. "I think it best that no one but you should hear anything of the matter for the present until I have investigated further. It was nearly half-past three this morning as I got around here on Five's post, inspecting sentinels, and came suddenly in the darkness upon a man carrying a ladder on his shoulder. I ordered him to halt. The reply was a violent blow, and the ladder and I were dropped at the same instant, while the man sprang into space and darted off in the direction of Number Five. I followed quick as I could, heard the challenge and the cries of halt, and shouted to Leary to fire. He did, but missed his aim in the haste and darkness, and the man got safely away. Of course there is much talk and speculation about it around the post this morning, for several people heard the shots besides the guard, and, although I told Leary and others to say nothing, I know it is already generally known."

"Oh, well, come in to breakfast," said the colonel. "We'll talk it over there."

"Pardon me, sir, I cannot. I must get back home before guard-mount, and Rollins is probably waiting to see me now. I—I could not discuss it at the table, for there are some singular features about the matter."

"Why, in God's name, what?" asked the colonel, with sudden and deep anxiety.

"Well, sir, an officer of the garrison is placed in a compromising position by this affair, and cannot or will not explain."

"Who?"

"Mr. Jerrold, sir."

"Jerrold! Why, I got a note from him not ten minutes ago saying he had an engagement in town and asking permission to go before guard-mounting, if Mr. Hall was ready. Hall wanted to go with him, Jerrold wrote, but Hall has not applied for permission to leave the post."

"It is Jerrold who is compromised, colonel. I may be all wrong in my suspicions, all wrong in reporting the matter to you at all, but in my perplexity and distress I see no other way. Frankly, sir, the moment I caught sight of the man he looked like Jerrold; and two minutes after the shots were fired I inspected Jerrold's quarters. He was not there, though the lamps were burning very low in the bedroom, and his bed had not been occupied at all. When you see Leary, sir, he will tell you that he also thought it must be Mr. Jerrold."

"The young scapegrace!—been off to town, I suppose."

"Colonel," said Chester, quickly, "you—not I—must decide that. I went to his quarters after reveille, and he was then there, and resented my visit and questions, admitted that he had been out during the night, but refused to make any statement to me."

"Well, Chester, I will haul him up after breakfast. Possibly he had been up to the rifle-camp, or had driven to town after the doctor's party. Of course *that* must be stopped; but I'm glad you missed him. It, of course, staggers a man's judgment to be knocked down, but if you had killed him it might have been as serious for you as this knock-down blow will be for him. That is the worst phase of the matter. What could he have been thinking of? He must have been either drunk or mad; and he rarely drank. Oh, dear, dear, dear, but that's very bad,—very bad,—striking the officer of the day! Why, Chester, that's the worst thing that's happened in the regiment since I took command of it. It's about the worst thing that *could* have happened to us. Of course he must go in arrest. I'll see the adjutant right after breakfast. I'll be over early, Chester." And with grave and worried face the colonel bade him adieu.

As he turned away, Chester heard him saying again to himself, "About the worst thing he could have done!—the worst thing he could have done!" And the captain's heart sank within him. What would the colonel say when he knew how far, far worse was the foul wrong Mr. Jerrold had done to him and his?

VII

Before guard-mounting—almost half an hour before his usual time for appearing at the office—Colonel Maynard hurried in to his desk, sent the orderly for Captain Chester, and then the clerks in the sergeant-major's room heard him close and lock the door. As the subject of the shooting was already under discussion among the men there assembled, this action on the part of the chief was considered highly significant. It was hardly five minutes before Chester came, looked surprised at finding the door locked, knocked, and was admitted.

The look on the haggard face at the desk, the dumb misery in the eyes, the wrath and horror in it all, carried him back twenty years to that gloomy morning in the casemates when the story was passed around that Captain Maynard had lost a wife and an intimate friend during the previous night. Chester saw at a glance that, despite his precautions, the blow had come, the truth been revealed at one fell swoop.

"Lock the door again, Chester, and come here. I have some questions to ask you."

The captain silently took the chair which was indicated by a wave of the colonel's hand, and waited. For a moment no word more was spoken. The old soldier, white and trembling strangely, reseated himself at the desk, and covered his face with his hands. Twice he drew them with feebly stroking movement over his eyes, as though to rally the stunned faculties and face the trying ordeal. Then a shiver passed through his frame, and with sudden lift of the head he fixed his gaze on Chester's face and launched the question,—

"Chester, is there any kindness to a man who has been through what I have in telling only half a tale, as you have done?"

The captain colored red. "I am at a loss to answer you, colonel," he said, after brief reflection. "You know far more than you did half an hour ago, and what I knew I could not bear to tell you as yet."

"My God! my God! Tell me *all*, and tell me at once. Here, man, if you need stimulant to your indignation and cannot speak without it, read this. I found it, open, among the rose-bushes in the garden, where she must have dropped it when out there with you. Read it. Tell me what it means; for, God knows, I can't believe such a thing of her."

He handed Chester a sheet of note-paper. It was moist and blurred on the first page, but the inner pages, though damp, were in good condition. The first, second, and third pages were closely covered in a bold, nervous hand that Chester knew well. It was Jerrold's writing, beyond a doubt, and Chester's face grew hot as he read, and his heart turned cold as stone when he finished the last hurried line.

"MY DARLING,—

"I *must* see you, if only for a moment, before you leave. Do not let this alarm you, for the more I think the more I am convinced it is only a bluff, but Captain Chester discovered my absence early this morning when spying around as usual, and now he claims to have knowledge of our secret. Even if he was on the terrace when I got back, it was too dark for him to recognize me, and it seems impossible that he can have got any real clue. He suspects, perhaps, and thinks to force me to confession; but I would guard your name with my life. Be wary. Act as though there were nothing on earth between us, and if we cannot meet until then I will be at the depot with the others to see you off, and will then have a letter ready with full particulars and instructions. It will be in the first thing I hand to you. Hide it until you can safely read it. Your mother must not be allowed a glimmer of suspicion, and then you are safe. As for me, even Chester cannot make the colonel turn against me now. My jealous one, my fiery sweetheart, do you not realize now that I was wise in showing her so much attention? A thousand kisses. Come what may, they cannot rob us of the past.

HOWARD.

"I fear you heard and were alarmed by the shots just after I left you. All was quiet when I got home."

It was some seconds before Chester could control himself sufficiently to speak. "I wish to God the bullet had gone through his heart!" he said.

"It has gone through mine,—through mine! This will kill her mother. Chester," cried the colonel, springing suddenly to his feet, "she must not know it. She must not dream of it. I tell you it would stretch her in the dust, *dead*, for she loves that child with all her strength, with all her being, I believe, for it is two mother-loves in one. She had a son, older than Alice by several years, her first-born,—her glory, he was,—but the boy inherited the father's passionate and impulsive nature.

He loved a girl utterly beneath him, and would have married her when he was only twenty. There is no question that he loved her well, for he refused to give her up, no matter what his father threatened. They tried to buy her off, and she scorned them. Then they had a letter written, while he was sent abroad under pretence that he should have his will if he came back in a year unchanged. By Jove, it seems she was as much in love as he, and it broke her heart. She went off and died somewhere, and he came back ahead of time because her letters had ceased, and found it all out. There was an awful scene. He cursed them both,—father and mother,—and left her senseless at his feet; and from that day to this they never heard of him, never could get the faintest report. It broke Renwick,—killed him, I guess, for he died in two years; and as for the mother, you would not think that a woman so apparently full of life and health was in desperate danger. She had some organic trouble with the heart years ago, they tell her, and this experience has developed it so that now any great emotion or sudden shock is perilous. Do you not see how doubly fearful this comes to us? Chester, I have weathered one awful storm, but I'm old and broken now. This—this beats me. Tell me what to do."

The captain was silent a few moments. He was thinking intently.

"Does she know you have that letter?" he asked.

Maynard shook his head: "I looked back as I came away. She was in the parlor, singing softly to herself, at the very moment I picked it up, lying open as it was right there among the roses, the first words staring me in the face. I meant not to read it,—never dreamed it was for her,—and had turned over the page to look for the superscription. There was none, but there I saw the signature and that postscript about the shots. That startled me, and I read it here just before you came, and then could account for your conduct,—something I could not do before. God of heaven! would any man believe it of her? It is incredible! Chester, tell me everything you know now,—even everything you suspect. I must see my way clear."

And then the captain, with halting and reluctant tongue, told his story: how he had stumbled on the ladder back of the colonel's quarters and learned from Number Five that some one had been prowling back of Bachelors' Row; how he returned there afterwards, found the ladder at the side-wall, and saw the tall form issue from her window; how he had given chase and been knocked breathless, and of his suspicions, and Leary's, as to the identity of the stranger.

The colonel bowed his head still deeper, and groaned aloud. But he had still other questions to ask.

"Did you see—any one else at the window?"

"Not while he was there."

"At any time, then,—before or after?" And the colonel's eyes would take no denial.

"I saw," faltered Chester, "nobody. The shade was pulled up while I was standing there, after I had tripped on the ladder. I supposed the noise of my stumble had awakened her."

"And was that all? Did you see nothing more?"

"Colonel, I *did* see, afterwards, a woman's hand and arm closing the shade."

"My God! And she told me she slept the night through,—never waked or heard a sound!"

"Did you hear nothing yourself, colonel?"

"Nothing. When she came home from the party she stopped a moment, saying something to him at the door, then came into the library and kissed me good-night. I shut up the house and went to bed about half-past twelve, and her door was closed when I went to our room."

"So there were two closed doors, yours and hers, and the broad hall between you?"

"Certainly. We have the doors open all night that lead into the rear rooms, and their windows. This gives us abundant air. Alice always has the hall door closed at night."

"And Mrs. Maynard,—was she asleep?"

"No. Mrs. Maynard was lying awake, and seemed a little restless and disturbed. Some of the women had been giving her some hints about Jerrold and fretting her. You know she took a strange fancy to him at the start. It was simply because he reminded her so strongly of the boy she had lost. She told me so. But after a little she began to discover traits in him she did not like, and then his growing intimacy with Alice worried her. She would have put a stop to the doctor's party,—to her going with him, I mean,—but the engagement was made some days ago. Two or three days since, she warned Alice not to trust him, she says; and it is really as much on this as any other account that we decided to get her away, off to see her aunt Grace. Oh, God! how blind we are! how blind we are!" And poor old Maynard bowed his head and almost groaned aloud.

Chester rose, and, in his characteristic way, began tramping nervously up and down. There was a knock at the door. "The adjutant's compliments, and 'twas time for guard-mount.

Would the colonel wish to see him before he went out?" asked the orderly.

"I ought to go, sir," said Chester. "I am old officer of the day, and there will be just time for me to get into full uniform."

"Let them go on without you," said Maynard. "I cannot spare you now. Send word to that effect. Now,—now about this man,—this Jerrold. What is the best thing we can do?—of course I know what he most deserves;—but what is the *best* thing under all the circumstances? Of course my wife and Alice will leave to-day. She was still sleeping when I left, and, pray God, is not dreaming of this. It was nearly two before she closed her eyes last night; and I, too, slept badly. You have seen him. What does he say?"

"Denies everything,—anything,—challenges me to prove that he was absent from his house more than five minutes,— indeed, I could not, for he may have come in just after I left,—and pretended utter ignorance of my meaning when I accused him of striking me before I ordered the sentry to fire. Of course it is all useless now. When I confront him with this letter he *must* give in. Then let him resign and get away as quietly as possible before the end of the week. No one need know the causes. Of course shooting is what he deserves; but shooting demands explanation. It is better for your name, hers, and all, that he should be allowed to live than that the truth were suspected, as it would be if he were killed. Indeed, sir, if I were you I would take them to Sablon, keep them away for a fortnight, and leave him to me. It may be even judicious to let him go on with all his duties as though nothing had happened, as though he had simply been absent from reveille, and let the whole matter drop like that until all remark and curiosity is lulled; then you can send her back to Europe or the East,—time enough to decide on that; but I will privately tell him he must quit the service in six months, and show him why. It isn't the way it ought to be settled; it probably isn't the way Armitage would do it; but it is the best thing that occurs to me. One thing is certain: you and they ought to get away at once, and he should not be permitted to see her again. I can run the post a few days and explain matters after you go."

The colonel sat in wretched silence a few moments; then he arose:

"If it were not for *her* danger,—her heart,—I would never drop the matter here,—never! I would see it through to the bitter end. But you are probably right as to the prudent course to take. I'll get them away on the noon train: he thinks they do not start until later. Now I must go and face it. My God, Chester! could you look at that child and realize it? Even now, even now, sir, I believe—I believe, someway—somehow—she is innocent."

"God grant it, sir!"

And then the colonel left the office, avoiding, as has been told, a word with any man. Chester buttoned the tell-tale letter in an inner pocket, after having first folded the sheet lengthwise and then enclosed it in a long official envelope. The officers, wondering at the colonel's distraught appearance, had come thronging in, hoping for information, and then had gone, unsatisfied and disgusted, practically turned out by their crabbed senior captain. The ladies, after chatting aimlessly about the quadrangle for half an hour, had decided that Mrs. Maynard must be ill, and, while most of them awaited the result, two of their number went to the colonel's house and rang at the bell. A servant appeared: "Mrs. Maynard wasn't very well this morning, and was break-fasting in her room, and Miss Alice was with her, if the ladies would please excuse them." And so the emissaries returned unsuccessful. Then, too, as we have seen, despite his good intention of keeping matters hushed as much as possible, Chester's nervous irritability had got the better of him, and he had made damaging admissions to Wilton of the existence of a cause of worriment and perplexity, and this Wilton told without compunction. And then there was another excitement, that set all tongues wagging. Every man had heard what Chester said, that Mr. Jerrold must not quit the garrison until he had first come and seen the temporary commanding officer, and Hall had speedily carried the news to his friend.

"Are *you* ready to go?" asked Mr. Jerrold, who was lacing his boots in the rear room.

"No. I've got to go and get into 'cits' first."

"All right. Go, and be lively! I'll wait for you at Murphy's, beyond the bridge, provided you say nothing about it."

"You don't mean you are going against orders?"

"Going? Of course I am. I've got old Maynard's permission, and if Chester means to revoke it he's got to get his adjutant here inside of ten seconds. What you tell me isn't official. I'm off *now*!"

And when the adjutant returned to Captain Chester it was with the information that he was too late: Mr. Jerrold's dog-cart had crossed the bridge five minutes earlier.

Perhaps an hour later the colonel sent for Chester, and the captain went to his house. The old soldier was pacing slowly up and down the parlor floor.

"I wanted you a moment. A singular thing has happened.

You know that 'Directoire' cabinet photo of Alice? My wife always kept it on her dressing-table, and this morning it's gone. That frame—the silver filigree thing—was found behind a sofa-pillow in Alice's room, and she declares she has no idea how it got there. Chester, is there any new significance in this?"

The captain bowed assent.

"What is it?"

"That photograph was seen by Major Sloat in Jerrold's bureau-drawer at reveille this morning."

And such was the situation at Sibley the August day the colonel took his wife and her lovely daughter to visit Aunt Grace at Lake Sablon.

VIII

In the big red omnibus that was slowly toiling over the dusty road several passengers were making their way from the railway-station to the hotel at Lake Sablon. Two of them were women of mature years, whose dress and bearing betokened lives of ease and comfort; another was a lovely brunette of less than twenty, the daughter, evidently, of one of these ladies, and an object of loving pride to both. These three seemed at home in their surroundings, and were absorbed in the packet of letters and papers they had just received at the station. It was evident that they were not new arrivals, as were the other passengers, who studied them with the half-envious feelings with which new-comers at a summer resort are apt to regard those who seem to have been long established there, and who gathered from the scraps of conversation that they had merely been over to say good-by to friends leaving on the very train which brought in the rest of what we good Americans term "the 'bus-load." There were women among the newly-arrived who inspected the dark girl with that calm, unflinching, impertinent scrutiny and half-audibly whispered comment which, had they been of the opposite sex, would have warranted their being kicked out of the conveyance, but which was ignored by the fair object and her friends as completely as were the commentators themselves. There were one or two men in the omnibus who might readily have been forgiven an admiring glance or two at so bright a vision of girlish beauty as was Miss Renwick this August afternoon, and they *had* looked; but the one who most attracted the notice of Mrs. Maynard and Aunt Grace—a tall, stalwart, distinguished-looking party in gray travelling-dress—had taken his seat close to the door and was deep in the morning's paper before they were fairly away from the station.

Laying down the letter she had just finished reading, Mrs. Maynard glanced at her daughter, who was still engaged in one of her own, and evidently with deep interest.

"From Fort Sibley, Alice?"

"Yes, mamma, all three,—Miss Craven, Mrs. Hoyt, and—Mr. Jerrold. Would you like to see it?" And, with rising color, she held forth the one in her hand.

"Not now," was the answer, with a smile that told of confidence and gratification both. "It is about the german, I suppose?"

"Yes. He thinks it outrageous that we should not be there,—says it is to be the prettiest ever given at the fort, and that Mrs. Hoyt and Mrs. Craven, who are the managers for the ladies, had asked him to lead. He wants to know if we cannot possibly come."

"Are you not very eager to go, Alice? I should be," said Aunt Grace, with sympathetic interest.

"Yes, I am," answered Miss Renwick, reflectively. "It had been arranged that it should come off next week, when, as was supposed, we would be home after this visit. It cannot be postponed, of course, because it is given in honor of all the officers who are gathered there for the rifle-competition, and that will be all over and done with to-day, and they cannot stay beyond Tuesday next. We must give it up, auntie," and she looked up smilingly, "and you have made it so lovely for me here that I can do it without a sigh. Think of that!—an army german!—and Fanny Craven says the favors are to be simply lovely. Yes, I *did* want to go, but papa said he felt unequal to it the moment he got back from Chicago, day before yesterday, and he certainly does not look at all well: so that ended it, and I wrote at once to Mrs. Hoyt. This is her answer now."

"What does she say?"

"Oh, it is very kind of her: she wants me to come and be her guest if the colonel is too ill to come and mamma will not leave him. She says Mr. Hoyt will come down and escort me. But I would not like to go without mamma," and the big dark eyes looked up wistfully, "and I know she does not care to urge papa when he seems so indisposed to going."

Mrs. Maynard's eyes were anxious and troubled now. She turned to her sister-in-law:

"Do you think he seems any better, Grace? I do not."

"It is hard to say. He was so nervously anxious to get away to see the general the very day you arrived here that there was not a moment in which I could ask him about himself; and since his return he has avoided all mention of it beyond saying it is nothing but indigestion and he would be all right in a few days. I never knew him to suffer in that way in my life. Is there any regimental matter that can be troubling him?" she asked, in lower tone.

"Nothing of any consequence whatever. Of course the officers feel chagrined over their defeat in the rifle-match.

They had expected to stand very high, but Mr. Jerrold's shooting was unexpectedly below the average, and it threw their team behind. But the colonel didn't make the faintest allusion to it. That hasn't worried him anywhere near as much as it has the others, I should judge."

"I do not think it was all Mr. Jerrold's fault, mamma," said Miss Renwick, with gentle reproach and a very becoming flush. "I'm going to stand up for him, because I think they all blame him for other men's poor work. He was not the only one on our team whose shooting was below former scores."

"They claim that none fell so far below their expectations as he, Alice. You know I am no judge of such matters, but Mr. Hoyt and Captain Gray both write the colonel that Mr. Jerrold had been taking no care of himself whatever and was entirely out of form."

"In any event I'm glad the cavalry did no better," was Miss Renwick's loyal response. "You remember the evening we rode out to the range and Captain Gray said that there was the man who would win the first prize from Mr. Jerrold,— that tall cavalry sergeant who fainted away,—Sergeant McLeod; don't you remember, mother? Well, he did not even get a place, and Mr. Jerrold beat him easily."

Something in her mother's eyes warned her to be guarded, and, in that indefinable but unerring system of feminine telegraphy, called her attention to the man sitting by the door. Looking quickly to her right, Miss Renwick saw that he was intently regarding her. At the mention of Fort Sibley the stranger had lowered his paper, revealing a bronzed face clean-shaven except for the thick blonde moustache, and a pair of clear, steady, searching blue eyes under heavy brows and lashes, and these eyes were very deliberately yet respectfully fixed upon her own; nor were they withdrawn in proper confusion when detected. It was Miss Renwick whose eyes gave up the contest and returned in some sense of defeat to her mother's face.

"What letters have you for the colonel?" asked Mrs. Maynard, coming *au secours*.

"Three,—two of them from his devoted henchman Captain Chester, who writes by every mail, I should imagine; and these he will go off into some secluded nook with and come back looking blue and worried. Then here's another, forwarded from Sibley, too. I do not know this hand. Perhaps it is from Captain Armitage, who, they say, is to come back next month. Poor Mr. Jerrold!"

"Why poor Mr. Jerrold?" asked Aunt Grace, with laughing interest, as she noted the expression on her niece's pretty face.

"Because he can't bear Captain Armitage, and—"

"Now, Alice!" said her mother, reprovingly. "You must not take his view of the captain at all. Remember what the colonel said of him—"

"Mother dear," protested Alice, laughing, "I have no doubt Captain Armitage is the paragon of a soldier, but he is unquestionably a most unpleasant and ungentlemanly person in his conduct to the young officers. Mr. Hall has told me the same thing. I declare, I don't see how they can speak to him at all, he has been so harsh and discourteous and unjust." The color was rising in earnest now, but a warning glance in her mother's eye seemed to check further words. There was an instant's silence. Then Aunt Grace remarked,—

"Alice, your next-door neighbor has vanished. I think your

vehemence has frightened him."

Surely enough, the big, blue-eyed man in tweeds had disappeared. During this brief controversy he had quickly and noiselessly let himself out of the open door, swung lightly to the ground, and was out of sight among the trees.

"Why, what a strange proceeding!" said Aunt Grace again. "We are fully a mile and a half from the hotel, and he means to walk it in this glaring sun."

Evidently he did. The driver reined up at the moment in response to a suggestion from some one in a forward seat, and there suddenly appeared by the wayside, striding out from the shelter of the sumachs, the athletic figure of the stranger.

"Go ahead!" he called, in a deep chest-voice that had an unmistakable ring to it,—the tone that one so readily recognizes in men accustomed to prompt action and command. "I'm going across lots." And, swinging his heavy stick, with quick, elastic steps and erect carriage the man in gray plunged into a wood-path and was gone.

"Alice," said Aunt Grace, again, "that man is an officer, I'm sure, and you have driven him into exile and lonely wandering. I've seen so much of them when visiting my brother in the old days before my marriage that even in civilian dress it is easy to tell some of them. Just look at that back, and those shoulders! He has been a soldier all his life. Horrors! suppose it should be Captain Armitage himself!"

Miss Renwick looked genuinely distressed, as well as vexed. Certainly no officer but Captain Armitage would have had reason to leave the stage. Certainly officers and their families occasionally visited Sablon in the summer-time, but Captain

Armitage could hardly be here. There was comforting assurance in the very note she held in her hand.

"It cannot be," she said, "because Mr. Jerrold writes that they have just heard from him at Sibley. He is still at the sea-shore, and will not return for a month. Mr. Jerrold says he implored Captain Chester to let him have three days' leave to come down here and have a sail and a picnic with us, and was told that it would be out of the question."

"Did he tell you any other news?" asked Mrs. Maynard, looking up from her letter again,—"anything about the german?"

"He says he thinks it a shame we are to be away and—well, read it yourself." And she placed it in her mother's hands, the dark eyes seriously, anxiously studying her face as she read. Presently Mrs. Maynard laid it down and looked again into her own, then, pointing to a certain passage with her finger, handed it to her daughter.

"Men were deceivers ever," she said, laughing, yet oracularly significant.

And Alice Renwick could not quite control the start with which she read,—

"Mr. Jerrold is to lead with his old love, Nina Beaubien. They make a capital pair, and she, of course, will be radiant—with Alice out of the way."

"That is something Mr. Jerrold failed to mention, is it not?"

Miss Renwick's cheeks were flushed, and the dark eyes were filled with sudden pain, as she answered,—

"I did not know she was there. She was to have gone to the Lakes the same day we left."

"She did go, Alice," said her mother, quietly, "but it was only for a brief visit, it seems."

The colonel was not at their cottage when the omnibus reached the lake. Over at the hotel were the usual number of loungers gathered to see the new arrivals, and Alice presently caught sight of the colonel coming through the park. If anything, he looked more listless and dispirited than he had before they left. She ran down the steps to meet him, smiling brightly up into his worn and haggard face.

"Are you feeling a little brighter, papa? Here are letters for you."

He took them wearily, barely glancing at the superscriptions.

"I had hoped for something more," he said, and passed on into the little frame house which was his sister's summer home. "Is your mother here?" he asked, looking back as he entered the door.

"In the north room, with Aunt Grace, papa," she answered; and then once more and with graver face she began to read Mr. Jerrold's letter. It was a careful study she was making of it this time, and not altogether a pleasant one. Aunt Grace came out and made some laughing remark at seeing her still so occupied. She looked up, pluckily smiling despite a sense of wounded pride, and answered,—

"I am only convincing myself that it was purely on general principles that Mr. Jerrold seemed so anxious I should be there. He never wanted me to lead with him at all." All the same it stung, and Aunt Grace saw and knew it, and longed to take her to her heart and comfort her; but it was better so. She was finding him out unaided.

She was still studying over portions of that ingenious letter, when the rustle of her aunt's gown indicated that she was rising. She saw her move towards the steps, heard a quick, firm tread upon the narrow planking, and glanced up in surprise. There, uncovering his close-cropped head, stood the tall stranger, looking placidly up as he addressed Aunt Grace:

"Pardon me, can I see Colonel Maynard?"

"He is at home. Pray come up and take a chair. I will let him know. I—I felt sure you must be some friend of his when I saw you in the stage," said the good lady, with manifest and apologetic uneasiness.

"Yes," responded the stranger, as he quickly ascended the steps and bowed before her, smiling quietly the while. "Let me introduce myself. I am Captain Armitage, of the colonel's regiment."

"There! I *knew* it!" was Aunt Grace's response, as with both hands uplifted in tragic despair she gave one horror-stricken glance at Alice and rushed into the house.

There was a moment's silence; then, with burning cheeks, but with brave eyes that looked frankly into his, Alice Renwick arose, came straight up to him, and held out her pretty hand.

"Captain Armitage, I beg your pardon."

He took the extended hand and gazed earnestly into her face, while a kind—almost merry—smile lighted up his own.

Charles King

"Have the boys given me such an uncanny reputation as all that?" he asked; and then, as though tickled with the comicality of the situation, he began to laugh. "What ogres some of us old soldiers do become in the course of years! Do you know, young lady, I might never have suspected what a brute I was if it had not been for you? What a blessed thing it was the colonel did not tell you I was coming! You would never have given me this true insight into my character."

But she saw nothing to laugh at, and would not laugh. Her lovely face was still burning with blushes and dismay and full of trouble.

"I do not look upon it lightly at all," she said. "It was unpardonable in me to—to—"

"To take so effective and convincing a method of telling a man of his grievous sins! Not a bit of it. I like a girl who has the courage to stand up for her friends. I shall congratulate Jerrold and Hall both when I get back, lucky fellows that they are!" And evidently Captain Armitage was deriving altogether too much jolly entertainment from her awkwardness. She rallied and strove to put an end to it.

"Indeed, Captain Armitage, I *do* think the young officers sorely need friends and advocates at times. I never would have knowingly spoken to you of your personal responsibilities in the woes of Mr. Jerrold and Mr. Hall, but since I have done so unwittingly I may as well define my position, especially as you are so good-natured with it all." And here, it must be admitted, Miss Renwick's beautiful eyes were shyly lifted to his in a most telling way. Once there, they looked squarely into the clear blue depths of his, and never flinched. "It seemed to me several times at Sibley that the young officers deserved more consideration and courtesy than their captains accorded them. It was not you alone that I heard of."

"I am profoundly gratified to learn that somebody else is a brute," he answered, trying to look grave, but with that irrepressible merriment twitching at the corners of his mouth and giving sudden gleams of his firm white teeth through the thick moustache. "You are come to us just in time, Miss Renwick, and if you will let me come and tell you all my sorrows the next time the colonel pitches into me for something wrong in B Company, I'll give you full permission to overhaul me for everything or anything I say and do to the youngsters. Is it a bargain?" And he held out his big, firm hand.

"I think you are—very different from what I heard," was all her answer, as she looked up in his eyes, twinkling as they were with fun. "Oh, we are to shake hands on it as a bargain? Is that it? Very well, then."

IX

When Captain Armitage left the cottage that night he did not go at once to his own room. Brief as was the conversation he had enjoyed with Miss Renwick, it was all that Fate vouchsafed him for that date at least. The entire party went to tea together at the hotel, but immediately thereafter the colonel carried Armitage away, and for two long hours they were closeted over some letters that had come from Sibley, and when the conference broke up and the wondering ladies saw the two men come forth it was late,—almost ten o'clock,—and the captain did not venture beyond the threshold of the sitting-room. He bowed and bade them a somewhat ceremonious good-night. His eyes rested— lingered—on Miss Renwick's uplifted face, and it was the picture he took with him into the stillness of the summer night.

The colonel accompanied him to the steps, and rested his hand upon the broad gray shoulder.

"God only knows how I have needed you, Armitage. This trouble has nearly crushed me, and it seemed as though I were utterly alone. I had the haunting fear that it was only weakness on my part and my love for my wife that made me stand out against Chester's propositions. He can only see guilt and conviction in every new phase of the case, and, though you see how he tries to spare me, his letters give no hope of any other conclusion."

Armitage pondered a moment before he answered. Then he slowly spoke:

"Chester has lived a lonely and an unhappy life. His first experience after graduation was that wretched affair of which you have told me. Of course I knew much of the particulars before, but not all. I respect Chester as a soldier and a gentleman, and I like him and trust him as a friend; but, Colonel Maynard, in a matter of such vital importance as this, and one of such delicacy, I distrust, not his motives, but his judgment. All his life, practically, he has been brooding over the sorrow that came to him when your trouble came to you, and his mind is grooved: he believes he sees mystery and intrigue in matters that others might explain in an instant."

"But think of all the array of evidence he has."

"Enough, and more than enough, I admit, to warrant every-thing he has thought or said of the man; but—"

"He simply puts it this way. If he be guilty, can she be less? Is it possible, Armitage, that you are unconvinced?"

"Certainly I am unconvinced. The matter has not yet been sifted. As I understand it, you have forbidden his confronting Jerrold with the proofs of his rascality until I get there. Admitting the evidence of the ladder, the picture, and the form at the window,—ay, the letter, too,—I am yet to be convinced of one thing. You must remember that his judgment is biassed by his early experiences. He fancies, that no woman is proof against such fascinations as Jerrold's."

"And your belief?"

"Is that some women—*many* women—are utterly above such a possibility."

Old Maynard wrung his comrade's hand. "You make me hope in spite of myself,—my past experiences,—my very senses, Armitage. I have leaned on you so many years that I missed you sorely when this trial came. If you had been there, things might not have taken this shape. He looks upon Chester—and it's one thing Chester hasn't forgiven in him— as a meddling old granny; you remember the time he so spoke of him last year; but he holds you in respect, or is afraid of you,—which in a man of his calibre is about the same thing. It may not be too late for you to act. Then when he is disposed of once and for all, I can know what must be done—where she is concerned."

"And under no circumstances can you question Mrs. Maynard?"

"No! no! If she suspected anything of this it would kill her. In any event, she must have no suspicion of it *now*."

"But does she not ask? Has she no theory about the missing photograph? Surely she must marvel over its disappearance."

"She *does*; at least, she *did*; but—I'm ashamed to own it, Armitage—we had to quiet her natural suspicions in some way, and I told her that it was my doing,—that I took it to tease Alice, put the photograph in the drawer of my desk, and hid the frame behind her sofa-pillow. Chester knows of the arrangement, and we had settled that when the picture was recovered from Mr. Jerrold he would send it to me."

Armitage was silent. A frown settled on his forehead, and it was evident that the statement was far from welcome to him. Presently he held forth his hand.

"Well, good-night, sir. I must go and have a quiet think over this. I hope you will rest well. You need it, colonel."

But Maynard only shook his head. His heart was too troubled for rest of any kind. He stood gazing out towards the park, where the tall figure of his ex-adjutant had disappeared among the trees. He heard the low-toned, pleasant chat of the ladies in the sitting-room, but he was in no mood to join them. He wished that Armitage had not gone, he felt such strength and comparative hope in his presence; but it was plain that even Armitage was confounded by the array of facts and circumstances that he had so painfully and slowly communicated to him. The colonel went drearily back to the room in which they had had their long conference. His wife and sister both hailed him as he passed the sitting-room door, and urged him to come and join them,—they wanted to ask about Captain Armitage, with whom it was evident they were much impressed; but he answered that he had some letters to put away, and he must attend first to that.

Among those that had been shown to the captain, mainly letters from Chester telling of the daily events at the fort and of his surveillance in the case of Jerrold, was one which Alice had brought him two days before. This had seemed to him of unusual importance, as the others contained nothing that tended to throw new light on the case. It said,—

"I am glad you have telegraphed for Armitage, and heartily approve your decision to lay the whole case before him. I presume he can reach you by Sunday, and that by Tuesday he will be here at the fort and ready to act. This will be a great relief to me, for, do what I could to allay it, there is no concealing the fact that much speculation and gossip is afloat concerning the events of that unhappy night. Leary declares he has been close-mouthed; the other men on guard know absolutely nothing, and Captain Wilton is the only officer to whom in my distress of mind I betrayed that there *was* a mystery, and he has pledged himself to me to say nothing. Sloat, too, has an inkling, and a big one, that Jerrold is the suspected party; but I never dreamed that anything had been seen or heard which in the faintest way connected *your* household with the matter, until yesterday. Then Leary admitted to me that two women, Mrs. Clifford's cook and the doctor's nursery-maid, had asked him whether it wasn't Lieutenant Jerrold he fired at, and if it was true that he was trying to get in at the colonel's back door. Twice Mrs. Clifford has asked me very significant questions, and three times to-day have officers made remarks to me that indicated their knowledge of the existence of some grave trouble. What makes matters worse is that Jerrold, when twitted about his absence from reveille, loses his temper and gets confused. There came near being a quarrel between him and Rollins at the mess a day or two since. He was saying that the reason he slept through roll-call was the fact that he had been kept up very late at the doctor's party, and Rollins happened to come in at the moment and blurted out that if he was up at all it must have been after he left the party, and reminded him that he had left before midnight with Miss Renwick. This completely staggered Jerrold, who grew confused and tried to cover it with a display of anger. Now, two weeks ago Rollins was most friendly to Jerrold and stood up for him when I assailed him, but ever since that night he has had no word to say for him. When Jerrold played wrathful and accused Rollins of mixing in other men's business, Rollins bounced up to him like a young bull-terrier, and I believe there would have been a row had not Sloat and Hoyt promptly interfered. Jerrold apologized, and Rollins accepted the apology, but has avoided him ever since,— won't speak of him to me, now that I have reason to want to draw him out. As soon as Armitage gets here he can do what I cannot,—find out just what and who is suspected and talked about.

"Mr. Jerrold, of course, avoids me. He has been attending strictly to his duty, and is evidently confounded that I did not press the matter of his going to town as he did the day I forbade it. Mr. Hoyt's being too late to see him personally gave me sufficient grounds on which to excuse it; but he seems to understand that something is impending, and is looking nervous and harassed. He has not renewed his request for leave of absence to run down to Sablon. I told him curtly it was out of the question."

The colonel took a few strides up and down the room. It had come, then. The good name of those he loved was already besmirched by garrison gossip, and he knew that nothing but heroic measures could ever silence scandal. Impulse and the innate sense of "fight" urged him to go at once to the scene, leaving his wife and her fair daughter here under his sister's roof; but Armitage and common sense said no. He had placed his burden on those broad gray shoulders, and, though ill content to wait, he felt that he was bound. Stowing away the letters, too nervous to sleep, too worried to talk, he stole from the cottage, and, with hands clasped behind his back, with low-bowed head he strolled forth into the broad vista of moonlit road.

There were bright lights still burning at the hotel, and gay voices came floating through the summer air. The piano, too, was thrumming a waltz in the parlor, and two or three couples were throwing embracing, slowly-twirling shadows on the windows. Over in the bar-and billiard-rooms the click of the balls and the refreshing rattle of cracked ice told suggestively of the occupation of the inmates. Keeping on beyond these distracting sounds, he slowly climbed a long, gradual ascent to the "bench," or plateau above the wooded point on which were grouped the glistening white buildings of the pretty summer resort, and, having reached the crest, turned silently to gaze at the beauty of the scene,—at the broad, flawless bosom of a summer lake all sheen and silver from the unclouded moon. Far to the southeast it wound among the bold and rock-ribbed bluffs rising from the forest growth at their base to shorn and rounded summits. Miles away to the southward twinkled the lights of one busy little town; others gleamed and sparkled over towards the northern shore, close under the pole-star; while directly opposite frowned a massive wall of palisaded rock, that threw, deep and heavy and far from shore, its long reflection in the mirror of water. There was not a breath of air stirring in the heavens, not a ripple on the face of the waters beneath, save where, close under the bold headland down on the other side, the signal-lights, white and crimson and green, creeping slowly along in the shadows, revealed one of the packets ploughing her steady way to the great marts below. Nearer at hand, just shaving the long strip of sandy, wooded point that jutted far out into the lake, a broad raft of timber, pushed by a hard-working, black-funnelled stern-wheeler, was slowly forging its way to the outlet of the lake, its shadowy edge sprinkled here and there with little sparks of lurid red,—the pilot-lights that gave warning of its slow and silent coming. Far down along the southern shore, under that black bluff-line, close to the silver water-edge, a glowing meteor seemed whirling through the night, and the low, distant rumble told of the "Atlantic Express" thundering on its journey. Here, along with him on the level plateau, were other roomy cottages, some dark, some still sending forth a guiding ray; while long lines of white-washed fence gleamed ghostly in the moonlight and were finally lost in the shadow of the great bluff that abruptly shut in the entire point and plateau and shut out all further sight of lake or land in that direction. Far beneath he could hear the soft plash upon the sandy shore of the little wavelets that came sweeping in the wake of the raft-boat and spending their tiny strength upon the strand; far down on the hotel point he could still hear the soft melody of the waltz; he remembered how the band used to play that same air, and wondered why it was he used to like it; it jarred him now. Presently the distant crack of a whip and the low rumble of wheels were heard: the omnibus coming back from the station with passengers from the night train. He was in no mood to see any one. He turned away and walked northward along the edge of the bench, towards the deep shadow of the great shoulder of the bluff, and presently he came to a long flight of wooden stairs, leading from the plateau down to the hotel, and here he stopped and seated himself awhile. He did not want to go home yet. He wanted to be by himself,—to think and brood over his trouble. He saw the omnibus go round the bend and roll up to the hotel door-way with its load of pleasure-seekers, and heard the joyous welcome with which some of their number were received by waiting friends, but life had little of joy to him this night. He longed to go away,—anywhere, anywhere, could he only leave this haunting misery behind. He was so proud of his regiment; he had been so happy in bringing home to it his accomplished and gracious wife; he had been so joyous in planning for the lovely times Alice was to have,—the social successes, the girlish triumphs, the garrison gayeties of which she was to be the queen,—and now, so very, very soon, all had turned to ashes and desolation! She *was* so beautiful, so sweet, winning, graceful. Oh, God! *could* it be that one so gifted could possibly be so base? He rose in nervous misery and clinched his hands high in air, then sat down again with hiding, hopeless face, rocking to and fro as sways a man in mortal pain. It was long before he rallied and again wearily arose. Most of the lights were gone; silence had settled down upon the sleeping point; he was chilled with the night air and the dew, and stiff and heavy as he tried to walk. Down at the foot of the stairs he could see the night-watchman making his rounds. He did not want to explain matters and talk with him: he would go around. There was a steep pathway down into the ravine that gave into the lake just beyond his sister's cottage, and this he sought and followed, moving slowly and painfully, but finally reaching the grassy level of the pathway that connected the cottages with the wood-road up the bluff. Trees and shrubbery were thick on both sides, and the path was shaded. He turned to his right, and came down until once more he was in sight of the white walls of the hotel standing out there on the point, until close at hand he could see the light of his own cottage glimmering like faithful beacon through the trees; and then he stopped short.

A tall, slender figure—a man in dark, snug-fitting clothing— was creeping stealthily up to the cottage window.

The colonel held his breath: his heart thumped violently: he waited,—watched. He saw the dark figure reach the blinds; he saw them slowly, softly turned, and the faint light gleaming from within; he saw the figure peering in between the slats, and then—God! was it possible?—a low voice, a man's voice, whispering or hoarsely murmuring a name: he heard a sudden movement within the room, as though the occupant had heard and were replying, "Coming." His blood froze: it was not Alice's room: it was his,—his and hers—his wife's,—and that was surely her step approaching the window. Yes, the blind was quickly opened. A white-robed figure stood at the casement. He could see, hear, bear no more: with one mad rush he sprang from his lair and hurled himself upon the shadowy stranger.

"You hound! who are you?"

But 'twas no shadow that he grasped. A muscular arm was round him in a trice, a brawny hand at his throat, a twisting, sinewy leg was curled in his, and he went reeling back upon the springy turf, stunned and wellnigh breathless.

When he could regain his feet and reach the casement the stranger had vanished; but Mrs. Maynard lay there on the floor within, a white and senseless heap.

X

Perhaps it was as well for all parties that Frank Armitage concluded that he must have another whiff of tobacco that night as an incentive to the "think" he had promised himself. He had strolled through the park to the grove of trees out on the point and seated himself in the shadows. Here his reflections were speedily interrupted by the animated flirtations of a few couples who, tiring of the dance, came out into the coolness of the night and the seclusion of the grove, where their murmured words and soft laughter soon gave the captain's nerves a strain they could not bear. He broke cover and betook himself to the very edge of the stone retaining wall out on the point.

He wanted to think calmly and dispassionately; he meant to weigh all he had read and heard and form his estimate of the gravity of the case before going to bed. He meant to be impartial,—to judge her as he would judge any other woman so compromised; but for the life of him he could not. He bore with him the mute image of her lovely face, with its clear, truthful, trustful dark eyes. He saw her as she stood before him on the little porch when they shook hands on their laughing— or his laughing—compact, for she would not laugh. How perfect she was!—her radiant beauty, her uplifted eyes, so full of their self-reproach and regret at the speech she had made at his expense! How exquisite was the grace of her slender, rounded form as she stood there before him, one slim hand half shyly extended to meet the cordial clasp of his own! He wanted to judge and be just; but that image dismayed him. How could he look on this picture and then—on that,—the one portrayed in the chain of circum-stantial evidence which the colonel had laid before him? It was monstrous! it was treason to womanhood! One look in her eyes, superb in their innocence, was too much for his determined impartiality. Armitage gave himself a mental kick for what he termed his imbecility, and went back to the hotel.

"It's no use," he muttered. "I'm a slave of the weed, and can't be philosophic without my pipe."

Up to his little box of a room he climbed, found his pipe-case and tobacco-pouch, and in five minutes was strolling out to the point once more, when he came suddenly upon the night-watchman,—a personage of whose functions and authority he was entirely ignorant. The man eyed him narrowly, and essayed to speak. Not knowing him, and desiring to be alone, Armitage pushed past, and was surprised to find that a hand was on his shoulder and the man at his side before he had gone a rod.

"Beg pardon, sir," said the watchman, gruffly, "but I don't know you. Are you stopping at the hotel?"

"I am," said Armitage, coolly, taking his pipe from his lips and blowing a cloud over his other shoulder. "And who may you be?"

"I am the watchman; and I do not remember seeing you come to-day."

"Nevertheless I did."

"On what train, sir?"

"This afternoon's up-train."

"You certainly were not on the omnibus when it got here."

"Very true. I walked over from beyond the school-house."

"You must excuse me, sir. I did not think of that; and the manager requires me to know everybody. Is this Major Armitage?"

"Armitage is my name, but I'm not a major."

"Yes, sir; I'm glad to be set right. And the other gentleman,—him as was inquiring for Colonel Maynard to-night? He's in the army, too, but his name don't seem to be on the book. He only came in on the late train."

"Another man to see Colonel Maynard?" asked the captain, with sudden interest. "Just come in, you say. I'm sure I've no idea. What was he like?"

"I don't know, sir. At first I thought you was him. The driver told me he brought a gentleman over who asked some questions about Colonel Maynard, but he didn't get aboard at the depot, and he didn't come down to the hotel,—got off somewhere up there on the bench, and Jim didn't see him."

"Where's Jim?" said Armitage. "Come with me, watchman. I want to interview him."

Together they walked over to the barn, which the driver was just locking up after making everything secure for the night.

"Who was it inquiring for Colonel Maynard?" asked Armitage.

"I don't know, sir," was the slow answer. "There was a man got aboard as I was coming across the common there in the village at the station. There were several passengers from the train, and some baggage: so he may have started ahead on foot but afterwards concluded to ride. As soon as I saw him get in I reined up and asked where he was going; he had no baggage nor nuthin', and my orders are not to haul anybody except people of the hotel: so he came right forward through the 'bus and took the seat behind me and said 'twas all right, he was going to the hotel; and he passed up a half-dollar. I told him that I couldn't take the money,—that 'bus-fares were paid at the office,—and drove ahead. Then he handed me a cigar, and pretty soon he asked me if there were many people, and who had the cottages; and when I told him, he asked which was Colonel Maynard's, but he didn't say he knew him, and the next thing I knew was when we got here to the hotel he wasn't in the 'bus. He must have stepped back through all those passengers and slipped off up there on the bench. He was in it when we passed the little brown church up on the hill."

"What was he like?"

"I couldn't see him plain. He stepped out from behind a tree as we drove through the common, and came right into the 'bus. It was dark in there, and all I know is he was tall and had on dark clothes. Some of the people inside must have seen him better; but they are all gone to bed, I suppose."

"I will go over to the hotel and inquire, anyway," said Armitage, and did so. The lights were turned down, and no one was there, but he could hear voices chatting in quiet tones on the broad, sheltered veranda without, and, going thither, found three or four men enjoying a quiet smoke. Armitage was a man of action. He stepped at once to the group:

"Pardon me, gentlemen, but did any of you come over in the omnibus from the station to-night?"

"I did, sir," replied one of the party, removing his cigar and twitching off the ashes with his little finger, then looking up with the air of a man expectant of question.

"The watchman tells me a man came over who was making inquiries for Colonel Maynard. May I ask if you saw or heard of such a person?"

"A gentleman got in soon after we left the station, and when the driver hailed him he went forward and took a seat near him. They had some conversation, but I did not hear it. I only know that he got out again a little while before we reached the hotel."

"Could you see him, and describe him? I am a friend of Colonel Maynard's, an officer of his regiment,—which will account for my inquiry."

"Well, yes, sir. I noticed he was very tall and slim, was dressed in dark clothes, and wore a dark slouched hat well down over his forehead. He was what I would call a military-looking man, for I noticed his walk as he got off; but he wore big spectacles,—blue or brown glass, I should say,—and had a heavy beard."

"Which way did he go when he left the 'bus?"

"He walked northward along the road at the edge of the bluff, right up towards the cottages on the upper level," was the answer.

Armitage thanked him for his courtesy, explained that he had left the colonel only a short time before and that he was then expecting no visitor, and if one had come it was perhaps necessary that he should be hunted up and brought to the hotel. Then he left the porch and walked hurriedly through the park towards its northernmost limit. There to his left stood the broad roadway along which, nestling under shelter of the bluff, was ranged the line of cottages, some two-storied, with balconies and verandas, others low, single-storied affairs with a broad hall-way in the middle of each and rooms on both north and south sides. Farthermost north on the row, almost hidden in the trees, and nearest the ravine, stood Aunt Grace's cottage, where were domiciled the colonel's household. It was in the big bay-windowed north room that he and the colonel had had their long conference earlier in the evening. The south room, nearly opposite, was used as their parlor and sitting-room. Aunt Grace and Miss Renwick slept in the little front rooms north and south of the hall-way, and the lights in their rooms were extinguished; so, too, was that in the parlor. All was darkness on the south and east. All was silence and peace as Armitage approached; but just as he reached the shadow of the stunted oak-tree growing in front of the house his ears were startled by an agonized cry, a woman's half-stifled shriek. He bounded up the steps, seized the knob of the door and threw his weight against it. It was firmly bolted within. Loud he thundered on the panels. "'Tis I,—Armitage!" he called. He heard the quick patter of little feet; the bolt was slid, and he rushed in, almost stumbling against a trembling, terror-stricken, yet welcoming white-robed form,—Alice Renwick, barefooted, with her glorious wealth of hair tumbling in dark luxuriance all down over the dainty night-dress,—Alice Renwick, with pallid face and wild imploring eyes.

"What is wrong?" he asked, in haste.

"It's mother,—her room,—and it's locked, and she won't answer," was the gasping reply.

Armitage sprang to the rear of the hall, leaned one second against the opposite wall, sent his foot with mighty impulse and muscled impact against the opposing lock, and the door flew open with a crash. The next instant Alice was bending over her senseless mother, and the captain was giving a hand in much bewilderment to the panting colonel, who was striving to clamber in at the window. The ministrations of Aunt Grace and Alice were speedily sufficient to restore Mrs. Maynard. A teaspoonful of brandy administered by the colonel's trembling hand helped matters materially. Then he turned to Armitage.

"Come outside," he said.

Once again in the moonlight the two men faced each other.

"Armitage, can you get a horse?"

"Certainly. What then?"

"Go to the station, get men, if possible, and head this fellow off. He was here again to-night, and it was not Alice he called, but my—but Mrs. Maynard. I saw him; I grappled with him right here at the bay-window where *she* met him, and he hurled me to grass as though I'd been a child. *I* want a horse! I want that man to-night. How did he get away from Sibley?"

"Do you mean—do you think it was Jerrold?"

"Good God, yes! Who else could it be? Disguised, of course, and bearded; but the figure, the carriage, were just the same, and he came to this window,—to *her* window,—and called, and she answered. My God, Armitage, think of it!"

"Come with me, colonel. You are all unstrung," was the captain's answer as he led his broken friend away. At the front door he stopped one moment, then ran up the steps and into the hall, where he tapped lightly at the casement.

"What is it?" was the low response from an invisible source.

"Miss Alice?"

"Yes."

"The watchman is here now. I will send him around to the window to keep guard until our return. The colonel is a little upset by the shock, and I want to attend to him. We are going to the hotel a moment before I bring him home. You are not afraid to have him leave you?"

"Not now, captain."

"Is Mrs. Maynard better?"

"Yes. She hardly seems to know what has happened. Indeed, none of us do. What was it?"

"A tramp, looking for something to eat, tried to open the blinds, and the colonel was out here and made a jump at him. They had a scuffle in the shrubbery, and the tramp got away. It frightened your mother: that's the sum of it, I think."

"Is papa hurt?"

"No: a little bruised and shaken, and mad as a hornet. I think perhaps I'll get him quieted down and sleepy in a few minutes, if you and Mrs. Maynard will be content to let him stay with me. I can talk almost any man drowsy."

"Mamma seems to worry for fear he is hurt."

"Assure her solemnly that he hasn't a scratch. He is simply fighting mad, and I'm going to try and find the tramp. Does Mrs. Maynard remember how he looked?"

"She could not see the face at all. She heard some one at the shutters, and a voice, and supposed of course it was papa, and threw open the blind."

"Oh, I see. That's all, Miss Alice. I'll go back to the colonel. Good-night!" And Armitage went forth with a lighter step.

"One sensation knocked endwise, colonel. I have it on the best of authority that Mrs. Maynard so fearlessly went to the window in answer to the voice and noise at the shutters simply because she knew you were out there somewhere and she supposed it was you. How simple these mysteries become when a little daylight is let in on them, after all! Come, I'm going to take you over to my room for a stiff glass of grog, and then after his trampship while you go back to bed."

"Armitage, you seem to make very light of this night's doings. What is easier than to connect it all with the trouble at Sibley?"

"Nothing was ever more easily explained than this thing, colonel, and all I want now is a chance to get that tramp. Then I'll go to Sibley; and 'pon my word I believe that mystery can be made as commonplace a piece of petty larceny as this was of vagrancy. Come."

But when Armitage left the colonel at a later hour and sought his own room for a brief rest he was in no such buoyant mood. A night-search for a tramp in the dense thickets among the bluffs and woods of Sablon could hardly be successful. It was useless to make the attempt. He slept but little during the cool August night, and early in the morning mounted a horse and trotted over to the railway-station.

"Has any train gone northward since last night?" he inquired at the office.

"None that stop here," was the answer. "The first train up comes along at 11.56."

"I want to send a despatch to Fort Sibley and get an answer without delay. Can you work it for me?"

The agent nodded, and pushed over a package of blanks. Armitage wrote rapidly as follows:

"CAPTAIN CHESTER,

"Commanding Fort Sibley.

"Is Jerrold there? Tell him I will arrive Tuesday. Answer.

"F. ARMITAGE."

It was along towards nine o'clock when the return message came clicking in on the wires, was written out, and handed to the tall soldier with the tired blue eyes.

He read, started, crushed the paper in his hand, and turned from the office. The answer was significant:

"Lieutenant Jerrold left Sibley yesterday afternoon. Not yet returned. Absent without leave this morning.

"CHESTER."

XI

Nature never vouchsafed to wearied man a lovelier day of rest than the still Sunday on which Frank Armitage rode slowly back from the station. The soft, mellow tone of the church-bell, tolling the summons for morning service, floated out from the brown tower, and was echoed back from the rocky cliff glistening in the August sunshine on the northern bluff. Groups of villagers hung about the steps of the little sanctuary and gazed with mild curiosity at the arriving parties from the cottages and the hotel. The big red omnibus came up with a load of worshippers, and farther away, down the vista of the road, Armitage could see others on foot and in carriages, all wending their way to church. He was in no mood to meet them. The story that he had been out pursuing a tramp during the night was pretty thoroughly circulated by this time, he felt assured, and every one would connect his early ride to the station, in some way, with the adventure that the grooms, hostlers, cooks, and kitchen-maids had all been dilating upon ever since daybreak. He dreaded to meet the curious glances of the women, and the questions of the few men whom he had taken so far into his confidence as to ask about the mysterious person who came over in the stage with them. He reined up his horse, and then, seeing a little pathway leading into the thick wood to his right, he turned in thither and followed it some fifty yards among bordering treasures of coreopsis and golden-rod and wild luxuriance of vine and foliage. Dismounting in the shade, he threw the reins over his arm and let his horse crop the juicy grasses, while he seated himself on a little stump and fell to thinking again. He could hear the reverent voices of one or two visitors strolling about among the peaceful, flower-decked graves behind the little church and only a short stone's-throw away through the shrubbery. He could hear the low, solemn voluntary of the organ, and presently the glad outburst of young voices in the opening hymn, but he knew that belated ones would still be coming to church, and he would not come forth from his covert until all were out of the way. Then, too, he was glad of a little longer time to think: he did not want to tell the colonel the result of his morning investigations.

To begin with: the watchman, the driver, and the two men whom he had questioned were all of an opinion as to the character of the stranger: "he was a military man." The passengers described his voice as that of a man of education and social position; the driver and passengers declared his walk and carriage to be that of a soldier: he was taller, they said, than the tall, stalwart Saxon captain, but by no means so heavily built. As to age, they could not tell: his beard was black and curly,—no gray hairs; his movements were quick and elastic; but his eyes were hidden by those colored glasses, and his forehead by the slouch of that broad-brimmed felt hat.

At the station, while awaiting the answer to his despatch, Armitage had questioned the agent as to whether any man of that description had arrived by the night train from the north. He had seen none, he said, but there was Larsen over at the post-office store, who came down on that train; perhaps he could tell. Oddly enough, Mr. Larsen recalled just such a party,—tall, slim, dark, dark-bearded, with blue glasses and dark hat and clothes,—but he was bound for Lakeville, the station beyond, and he remained in the car when he, Larsen, got off. Larsen remembered the man well, because he sat in the rear corner of the smoker and had nothing to say to anybody, but kept reading a newspaper; and the way he came to take note of him was that while standing with two friends at that end of the car they happened to be right around the man. The Saturday evening train from the city is always crowded with people from the river towns who have been up to market or the *matinees*, and even the smoker was filled with standing men until they got some thirty miles down. Larsen wanted to light a fresh cigar, and offered one to each of his friends: then it was found they had no matches, and one of them, who had been drinking a little and felt jovial, turned to the dark stranger and asked him for a light, and the man, without speaking, handed out a little silver match-box. It was just then that the conductor came along, and Larsen saw his ticket. It was a "round trip" to Lakeville: he was evidently going there for a visit, and therefore, said Larsen, he didn't get off at Sablon Station, which was six miles above.

But Armitage knew better. It was evident that he had quietly slipped out on the platform of the car after the regular passengers had got out of the way, and let himself off into the darkness on the side opposite the station. Thence he had an open and unimpeded walk of a few hundred yards until he reached the common, and then, when overtaken by the hotel omnibus, he could jump aboard and ride. There was only one road, only one way over to the hotel, and he could not miss it. There was no doubt now that, whoever he was, the night visitor had come down on the evening train from the city; and his return ticket would indicate that he meant to go back the way he came. It was half-past ten when that train arrived. It was nearly midnight when the man appeared at the cottage window. It was after two when Armitage gave up the search and went to bed. It was possible for the man to have walked to Lakeville, six miles south, and reached the station there in abundant time to take the up-train which passed Sablon, without stopping, a little before daybreak. If he took that train, and if he was Jerrold, he would have been in the city before seven, and could have been at Fort Sibley before or by eight o'clock. But Chester's despatch showed clearly that at 8.30—the hour for signing the company morning reports—Mr. Jerrold was not at his post. Was he still in the neighborhood and waiting for the noon train? If so, could he be confronted on the cars and accused of his crime? He looked at his watch; it was nearly eleven, and he must push on to the hotel before that hour, report to the colonel, then hasten back to the station. He sprang to his feet, and was just about to mount, when a vision of white and scarlet came suddenly into view. There, within twenty feet of him, making her dainty way through the shrubbery from the direction of the church, sunshine and shadow alternately flitting across her lovely face and form, Alice Renwick stepped forth into the pathway, and, shading her eyes with her hand, gazed along the leafy lane towards the road, as though expectant of another's coming. Then, attracted by the beauty of the golden-rod, she bent and busied herself with gathering in the yellow sprays. Armitage, with one foot in the stirrup, stood stock-still, half in surprise, half stunned by a sudden and painful thought. Could it be that she was there in hopes of meeting—any one?

He retook his foot from the stirrup, and, relaxing the rein, still stood gazing at her over his horse's back. That placid quadruped, whose years had been spent in these pleasant by-ways and were too many to warrant an exhibition of coltish surprise, promptly lowered his head and resumed his occupation of grass-nibbling, making a little crunching noise which Miss Renwick might have heard, but apparently did not. She was singing very softly to herself,—

"Daisy, tell my fortune, pray:
He loves me not,—he loves me."

And still Armitage stood and gazed, while she, absorbed in her pleasant task, still pulled and plucked at the golden-rod. In all his life no "vision of fair women" had been to him fair and sacred and exquisite as this. Down to the tip of her arched and slender foot, peeping from beneath the broidered hem of her snowy skirt, she stood the lady born and bred, and his eyes looked on and worshipped her,—worshipped, yet questioned, Why came she here? Absorbed, he released his hold on the rein, and Dobbin, nothing loath, reached with his long, lean neck for further herbage, and stepped in among the trees. Still stood his negligent master, fascinated in his study of the lovely, graceful girl. Again she raised her head and looked northward along the winding, shaded wood-path. A few yards away were other great clusters of the wild flowers she loved, more sun-kissed golden-rod, and, with a little murmur of delight, gathering her dainty skirts in one hand, she flitted up the pathway like an unconscious humming-bird garnering the sweets from every blossom. A little farther on the pathway bent among the trees, and she would be hidden from his sight; but still he stood and studied her every movement, drank in the soft, cooing melody of her voice as she sang, and then there came a sweet, solemn strain from the brown, sunlit walls just visible through the trees, and reverent voices and the resonant chords of the organ thrilled through the listening woods the glorious anthem of the church militant.

At the first notes she lifted up her queenly head and stood, listening and appreciative. Then he saw her rounded throat swelling like a bird's, and the rich, full tones of her voice rang out through the welcoming sunshine, and the fluttering wrens, and proud red-breasted robins, and rival song-queens, the brown-winged thrushes,—even the impudent shrieking jays,—seemed to hush and listen. Dobbin, fairly astonished, lifted up his hollow-eyed head and looked amazedly at the white songstress whose scarlet sash and neck-ribbons gleamed in such vivid contrast to the foliage about her. A wondering little "cotton-tail" rabbit, shy and wild as a hawk, came darting through the bushes into the sunshiny patchwork on the path, and then, uptilted and with quivering ears and nostrils and wide-staring eyes, stood paralyzed with helpless amaze, ignoring the tall man in gray as did the singer herself. Richer, rounder, fuller grew the melody, as, abandoning herself to the impulse of the sacred hour, she joined with all her girlish heart in the words of praise and thanksgiving,—in the glad and triumphant chorus of the Te Deum. From beginning to end she sang, now ringing and exultant, now soft and plaintive, following the solemn words of the ritual,—sweet and low and suppliant in the petition, "We therefore pray Thee help Thy servants whom Thou hast redeemed with Thy precious blood," confident and exulting in the declaration, "Thou art the King of Glory, O Christ," and then rich with fearless trust and faith in the thrilling climax, "Let me never be confounded." Armitage listened as one in a trance. From the depth of her heart the girl had joined her glorious voice to the chorus of praise and adoration, and now that all was stilled once more her head had fallen forward on her bosom, her hands, laden with golden-rod, were joined together: it seemed as though she were lost in prayer.

And this was the girl, this the pure, God-worshipping, God-fearing woman, who for one black instant he had dared to fancy had come here expectant of a meeting with the man whose aim had been frustrated but the night before! He could have thrown himself at her feet and implored her pardon. He *did* step forth, and then, hat in hand, baring his proud Saxon head as his forefathers would have uncovered to their monarch, he waited until she lifted up her eyes and saw him, and knew by the look in his frank face that he had stood by, a mute listener to her unstudied devotions. A lovely flush rose to her very temples, and her eyes drooped their pallid lids until the long lashes swept the crimson of her cheeks.

"Have *you* been here, captain? I never saw you," was her fluttering question.

"I rode in here on my way back from the station, not caring to meet all the good people going to church. I felt like an outcast."

"I, too, am a recreant to-day. It is the first time I have missed service in a long while. Mamma felt too unstrung to come, and I had given up the idea, but both she and Aunt Grace urged me. I was too late for the omnibus, and walked up, and then I would not go in because service was begun, and I wanted to be home again before noon. I cannot bear to be late at church, or to leave it until everything is over, but I can't be away from mother so long to-day. Shall we walk that way now?"

"In a minute. I must find my horse. He is in here somewhere. Tell me how the colonel is feeling, and Mrs. Maynard."

"Both very nervous and worried, though I see nothing extraordinary in the adventure. We read of poor hungry tramps everywhere, and they rarely do harm."

"I wonder a little at your venturing here in the wood-paths, after what occurred last night."

"Why, Captain Armitage, no one would harm me here, so close to the church. Indeed, I never thought of such a thing until you mentioned it. Did you discover anything about the man?"

"Nothing definite; but I must be at the station again to meet the up-train, and have to see the colonel meantime. Let me find Dobbin, or whatever they call this venerable relic I'm riding, and then I'll escort you home."

But Dobbin had strayed deeper into the wood. It was some minutes before the captain could find and catch him. The rich melody of sacred music was again thrilling through the perfumed woods, the glad sunshine was pouring its warmth and blessing over all the earth, glinting on bluff and brake and palisaded cliff, the birds were all singing their rivalling psaltery, and Nature seemed pouring forth its homage to the Creator and Preserver of all on this His holy day, when Frank Armitage once more reached the bowered lane where, fairest, sweetest sight of all, his lady stood waiting him. She turned to him as she heard the hoof-beat on the turf, and smiled.

"Can we wait and hear that hymn through?"

"Ay. Sing it."

She looked suddenly in his face. Something in the very tone in which he spoke startled her,—something deeper, more fervent, than she had ever heard before,—and the expression in the steady, deep-blue eyes was another revelation. Alice Renwick had a woman's intuition, and yet she had not known this man a day. The color again mounted to her temples, and her eyes fell after one quick glance.

"I heard you joining in the Te Deum," he urged. "Sing once more: I love it. There, they are just beginning again. Do you know the words?"

She nodded, then raised her head, and her glad young voice carolled through the listening woods:

"Holy, holy, holy! All
Heaven's triumphant choir shall sing,
When the ransomed nations fall
At the footstool of their King:
Then shall saints and seraphim,
Hearts and voices, swell one hymn
Round the throne with full accord,
Holy, holy, holy Lord!"

There was silence when the music ceased. She had turned
her face towards the church, and, as the melody died away in
one prolonged, triumphant chord, she still stood in reverent
attitude, as though listening for the words of benediction. He,
too, was silent, but his eyes were fixed on her. He was thirty-
five, she not twenty. He had lived his soldier life wifeless,
but, like other soldiers, his heart had had its rubs and aches
in the days gone by. Years before he had thought life a black
void when the girl he fancied while yet he wore the
Academic gray calmly told him she preferred another. Nor
had the intervening years been devoid of their occasional
yearnings for a mate of his own in the isolation of the
frontier or the monotony of garrison life; but flitting fancies
had left no trace upon his strong heart. The love of his life
only dawned upon him at this late day when he looked into
her glorious eyes and his whole soul went out in passionate
worship of the fair girl whose presence made that sunlit lane
a heaven. Were he to live a thousand years, no scene on earth
could rival in his eyes the love-haunted woodland pathway
wherein like forest queen she stood, the sunshine and leafy
shadows dancing over her graceful form, the golden-rod
enhancing her dark and glowing beauty, the sacred influ-
ences of the day throwing their mystic charm about her as
though angels guarded and shielded her from harm. His life
had reached its climax; his fate was sealed; his heart and soul
were centred in one sweet girl,—and all in one brief hour in
the woodland lane at Sablon.

She could not fail to see the deep emotion in his eyes as at last she turned to break the silence.

"Shall we go?" she said, simply.

"It is time; but I wish we could remain."

"You do not go to church very often at Sibley, do you?"

"I have not, heretofore; but you would teach me to worship." "You *have* taught me," he muttered below his breath, as he extended a hand to assist her down the sloping bank towards the avenue. She looked up quickly once more, pleased, yet shy, and shifted her great bunch of golden-rod so that she could lay her hand in his and lean upon its steady strength down the incline; and so, hand in hand, with old Dobbin ambling placidly behind, they passed out from the shaded pathway to the glow and radiance of the sunlit road.

XII

"Colonel Maynard, I admit everything you say as to the weight of the evidence," said Frank Armitage, twenty minutes later, "but it is my faith—understand me: my *faith*, I say—that she is utterly innocent. As for that damnable letter, I do not believe it was ever written to her. It is some other woman."

"What other is there, or was there?" was the colonel's simple reply.

"That is what I mean to find out. Will you have my baggage sent after me to-night? I am going at once to the station, and thence to Sibley. I will write you from there. If the midnight visitor should prove to have been Jerrold, he can be made to explain. I have always held him to be a conceited fop, but never either crack-brained or devoid of principle. There is no time for explanation *now*. Good-by; and keep a good lookout. That fellow may be here again."

And in an hour more Armitage was skimming along the winding river-side *en route* to Sibley. He had searched the train from pilot to rear platform, and no man who in the faintest degree resembled Mr. Jerrold was on board. He had wired to Chester that he would reach the fort that evening, but would not resume duty for a few days. He made another search through the train as they neared the city, and still there was no one who in stature or appearance corresponded with the descriptions given him of the sinewy visitor.

Late in the afternoon Chester received him as he alighted from the train at the little station under the cliff. It was a beautiful day, and numbers of people were driving or riding out to the fort, and the high bridge over the gorge was constantly resounding to the thunder of hoofs. Many others, too, had come out on the train; for the evening dress-parade always attracted a swarm of visitors. A corporal of the guard, with a couple of men, was on hand to keep vigilant eye on the arrivals and to persuade certain proscribed parties to re-enter the cars and go on, should they attempt to revisit the post, and the faces of these were lighted up as they saw their old adjutant; but none others of the garrison appeared.

"Let us wait a moment and get these people out of the way," said Armitage. "I want to talk with you. Is Jerrold back?"

"Yes. He came in just ten minutes after I telegraphed to you, was present at inspection, and if it had not been for your despatch this morning I should not have known he had remained out of quarters. He appeared to resent my having been to his quarters,—calls it spying, I presume."

"What permission had he to be away?"

"I gave him leave to visit town on personal business yesterday afternoon. He merely asked to be away a few hours to meet friends in town, and Mr. Hall took tattoo roll-call for him. As I do not require any other officer to report the time of his return, I did not exact it of him; but of course no man can be away after midnight without special permission, and he was gone all night. What is it, Armitage? Has he followed her down there?"

"Somebody was there last night and capsized the colonel pretty much as he did you the night of the ladder episode," said Armitage, coolly.

"By heaven! and I let him go!"

"How do you know 'twas he?"

"Who else could it be, Armitage?"

"That's what the colonel asks; but it isn't clear to me yet awhile."

"I wish it were less clear to me," said Chester, gloomily. "The worst is that the story is spreading like a pestilence all over the post. The women have got hold of it, and there is all manner of talk. I shouldn't be surprised if Mrs. Hoyt had to be taken violently ill. She has written to invite Miss Renwick to visit her, as it is certain that Colonel and Mrs. Maynard cannot come, and Hoyt came to me in a horror of amaze yesterday to know if there were any truth in the rumor that I had caught a man coming out of Mrs. Maynard's window the other night. I would tell him nothing, and he says the ladies declare they won't go to the german if *she* does. Heavens! I'm thankful you are come. The thing has been driving me wild these last twelve hours. I wanted to go away myself. *Is* she coming up?"

"No, she isn't; but let me say this, Chester: that whenever she is ready to return I shall be ready to escort her."

Chester looked at his friend in amazement, and without speaking.

"Yes, I see you are astonished, but you may as well understand the situation. I have heard all the colonel could tell, and have even seen the letter, and since she left here a mysterious stranger has appeared by night at Sablon, at the cottage window, though it happened to be her mother's this time, and I don't believe Alice Renwick knows the first thing about it."

"Armitage, are you in love?"

"Chester, I am in my sound senses. Now come and show me the ladder, and where you found it, and tell me the whole story over again. I think it grows interesting. One moment: has he that picture yet?"

"I suppose so. I don't know. In these last few days everybody is fighting shy of him. He thinks it is my doing, and looks black and sulky at me, but is too proud or too much afraid of consequences to ask the reason of the cold shoulders and averted looks. Gray has taken seven days' leave and gone off with that little girl of his to place her with relatives in the East. He has heard the stories, and it is presumed that some of the women have told her. She was down sick here a day or two."

"Well, now for the window and the ladder. I want to see the outside through your eyes, and then I will view the interior with my own. The colonel bids me do so."

Together they slowly climbed the long stairway leading up the face of the cliff. Chester stopped for a breathing-spell more than once.

"You're all out of condition, man," said the younger captain, pausing impatiently. "What has undone you?"

"This trouble, and nothing else. By gad! it has unstrung the whole garrison, I believe. You never saw our people fall off so in their shooting. Of course we expected Jerrold to go to pieces, but nobody else."

"There were others that seemed to fall away, too. Where was that cavalry-team that was expected to take the skirmish medal away from us?"

"Sound as a dollar, every man, with the single exception of their big sergeant. I don't like to make ugly comparisons to a man whom I believe to be more than half interested in a woman, but it makes me think of the old story about Medusa. One look at her face is too much for a man. That Sergeant McLeod went to grass the instant he caught sight of her, and never has picked up since."

"Consider me considerably more than half interested in the woman in this case, Chester: make all the comparisons that you like, provided they illumine matters as you are doing now, and tell me more of this Sergeant McLeod. What do you mean by his catching sight of her and going to grass?"

"I mean he fell flat on his face the moment he saw her, and hasn't been in good form from that moment to this. The doctor says it's heart-disease."

"That's what the colonel says troubles Mrs. Maynard. She was senseless and almost pulseless some minutes last night. What manner of man is McLeod?"

"A tall, slim, dark-eyed, swarthy fellow,—a man with a history and a mystery, I judge."

"A man with a history,—a mystery,—who is tall, slim, has dark eyes and swarthy complexion, and faints away at sight of Miss Renwick, might be said to possess peculiar characteristics,—family traits, some of them. Of course you've kept an eye on McLeod. Where is he?"

Chester stood leaning on the rail, breathing slowly and heavily. His eyes dilated as he gazed at Armitage, who was surveying him coolly, though the tone in which he spoke betrayed a new interest and a vivid one.

"I confess I never thought of him in connection with this affair," said Chester.

"There's the one essential point of difference between us," was the reply. "You go in on the supposition that there is only one solution to this thing, and that a woman must be dishonored to begin with. I believe there can be several solutions, and that there is only one thing in the lot that is at all impossible."

"What's that?"

"Miss Renwick's knowledge of that night's visitor, or of any other secret or sin. I mean to work other theories first; and the McLeod trail is a good one to start on. Where can I get a look at him?"

"Somewhere out in the Rockies by this time. He was ordered back to his troop five days ago, and they are out scouting at this moment, unless I'm vastly mistaken. You have seen the morning despatches?"

"About the Indians? Yes. Looks squally at the Spirit Rock reservation. Do you mean that McLeod is there?"

"That's where his troop ought to be by this time. There is too small a force on the trail now, and more will have to go if a big outbreak is to be prevented."

"Then he has gone, and I cannot see him. Let me look at the window, then."

A few steps brought them to the terrace, and there, standing by the west wall and looking up at the closed slats of the dormer-window, Captain Chester retold the story of his night-adventure. Armitage listened attentively, asking few questions. When it was finished, the latter turned and walked to the rear door, which opened on the terrace. It was locked.

"The servants are having a holiday, I presume," he said. "So much the better. Ask the quartermaster for the key of the front door, and I'll go in while everybody is out looking at dress-parade. There goes first call now. Let your orderly bring it to me here, will you?"

Ten minutes later, with beating heart, he stood and uncovered his handsome head and gazed silently, reverently around him. He was in her room.

It was dainty as her own dainty self. The dressing-table, the windows, the pretty little white bed, the broad, inviting lounge, the work-table and basket, the very wash-stand, were all trimmed and decked alike,—white and yellow prevailing. White lace curtains draped the window on the west—that fateful window—and the two that opened out on the roof of the piazza. White lace curtains draped the bed, the dressing-table, and the wash-stand; white lace, or some equally flimsy and feminine material, hung about her book-shelves and work-table and over the lounge; and bows of bright yellow ribbon were everywhere, yellow pin-cushions and wall-pockets hung about the toilet-table, soft yellow rugs lay at the bed-and lounge-side, and a sunshiny tone was given to the whole apartment by the shades of yellow silk that hung close to the windows.

On the wall were some choice etchings and a few foreign photographs. On the book-shelves were a few volumes of poetry, and the prose of George Eliot and our own Hawthorne. Hanging on pegs in the corner of the simple army room, covered by a curtain, were some heavy outer-garments,—an ulster, a travelling coat and cape of English make, and one or two dresses that were apparently too thick to be used at this season of the year. He drew aside the curtain one moment, took a brief glance at the garments, raised the hem of a skirt to his lips, and turned quickly away. A door led from the room to the one behind it,—a spare bedroom, evidently, that was lighted only from the back of the house and had no side-window at all. Another door led to the hall, a broad, old-fashioned affair, and crossing this he stood in the big front room occupied by the colonel and his wife. This was furnished almost as luxuriously (from an army point of view) as that of Miss Renwick, but not in white and yellow. Armitage smiled to see the evidences of Mrs. Maynard's taste and handiwork on every side. In the years he had been the old soldier's adjutant nothing could have exceeded the simplicity with which the colonel surrounded himself. Now it was something akin to Sybaritish elegance, thought the captain; but all the same he made his deliberate survey. There was the big dressing-table and bureau on which had stood that ravished picture,—that photograph of the girl he loved which others were able to speak of, and one man to appropriate feloniously, while yet he had never seen it. His impulse was to go to Jerrold's quarters and take him by the throat and demand it of him; but what right had he? How knew he, even, that it was now there? In view of the words that Chester had used towards him, Jerrold must know of the grievous danger in which he stood. That photograph would prove most damaging evidence if discovered. Very probably, after yielding to his vanity and showing it to Sloat he meant to get it back. Very certainly, after hearing Chester's words he must have determined to lose no time in getting rid of it. He was no fool, if he was a coxcomb.

Looking around the half-darkened room, Armitage lingered long over the photographs which hung about the dressing-table and over the mantel,—several prettily-framed duplicates of those already described as appearing in the album. One after another he took them in his hands, bore them to the window, and studied them attentively: some were not replaced without a long, lingering kiss. He had not ventured to disturb an item in her room. He would not touch the knob of a drawer or attempt to open anything she had closed, but here in quarters where his colonel could claim joint partnership he felt less sentiment or delicacy. He closed the hall door and tried the lock, turning the knob to and fro. Then he reopened the door and swung it upon its hinges. For a wonder, neither lock nor hinges creaked. The door worked smoothly and with little noise. Then he similarly tried the door of her room. It was in equally good working order,— quite free from the squeak and complaint with which quartermasters' locks and hinges are apt to do their reluctant duty. The discovery pleased him. It was possible for one to open and close these portals noiselessly, if need be, and without disturbing sleepers in either room. Returning to the east chamber, he opened the shades, so as to get more light, and his eye fell upon an old album lying on a little table that stood by the bedside. There was a night-lamp upon the table, too,—a little affair that could hold only a thimbleful of oil and was intended, evidently, to keep merely a faint glow during the night hours. Other volumes—a Bible, some devotional books, like "The Changed Cross," and a Hymnal or two—were also there; but the album stood most promi-nent, and Armitage curiously took it up and opened it.

There were only half a dozen photographs in the affair. It was rather a case than an album, and was intended apparently for only a few family pictures. There was but one that interested him, and this he examined intently, almost excitedly. It represented a little girl of nine or ten years,— Alice, undoubtedly,—with her arms clasped about the neck of a magnificent St. Bernard dog and looking up into the handsome features of a tall, slender, dark-eyed, black-haired boy of sixteen or thereabouts; and the two were enough alike to be brother and sister. Who, then, was this boy?

Armitage took the photograph to the window and studied it carefully. Parade was over, and the troops were marching back to their quarters. The band was playing gloriously as it came tramping into the quadrangle, and the captain could not but glance out at his own old company as in compact column of fours it entered the grassy diamond and swung off towards the barracks. He saw a knot of officers, too, turning the corner by the adjutant's office, and for a moment he lowered the album to look. Mr. Jerrold was not of the number that came sauntering up the walk, dropping away by ones or twos as they reached their doors and unbuckled their belts or removed their helmets in eager haste to get out of the constraint of full dress. But in another moment Jerrold, too, appeared, all alone, walking rapidly and nervously. Armitage watched him, and could not but see how other men turned away or gave him the coolest possible nod as he passed. The tall, slender lieutenant was handsomer even than when he last saw him; and yet there was gloom and worry on the dark beauty of his face. Nearer and nearer he came, and had passed the quarters of the other officers and was almost at the door of his own, when Armitage saw a little, wiry soldier in full dress uniform running across the parade as though in pursuit. He recognized Merrick, one of the scapegraces of his company, and wondered why he should be chasing after his temporary commander. Just as Jerrold was turning under the piazza the soldier seemed to make himself heard, and the lieutenant, with an angry frown on his face, stopped and confronted him.

"I told you not to come to me again," he said, so loud that every word was audible to the captain standing by the open window above. "What do you mean, sir, by following me in this way?"

The reply was inaudible. Armitage could see the little soldier standing in the respectful position of "attention," looking up and evidently pleading.

"I won't do it until I'm ready," was again heard in Jerrold's angry tones, though this time the lieutenant glanced about, as though to see if others were within earshot. There was no one, apparently, and he grew more confident. "You've been drinking again to-day, Merrick; you're not sober now; and I won't give you money to get maudlin and go to blabbing secrets on. No, sir! Go back to your quarters, and stay there."

The little soldier must indeed have been drinking, as the lieutenant declared. Armitage saw that he hesitated, instead of obeying at once, and that his flushed face was angrily working, then that he was arguing with his superior and talking louder. This was contrary to all the captain's ideas of proper discipline, even though he was indignant at the officer for permitting himself to be placed in so false and undignified a position. Jerrold's words, too, had acquired a wide significance; but they were feeble as compared with the sudden outburst that came from the soldier's lips:

"By God, lieutenant, you bribed me to silence to cover your tracks, and then you refuse to pay. If you don't want me to tell what I know, the sooner you pay that money the better."

This was more than Armitage could stand. He went downstairs three at a jump and out through the colonel's garden with quick, impetuous steps. Jerrold's furious face turned ashen at the sight, and Merrick, with one amazed and frightened look at his captain, faced about and slunk silently away. To him Armitage paid no further attention. It was to the officer he addressed himself:

"Mr. Jerrold, I have heard pretty much all this conversation. It simply adds to the evil report with which you have managed to surround yourself. Step into your quarters. I must see you alone."

Jerrold hesitated. He was thunderstruck by the sudden appearance of the captain whom he had believed to be hundreds of miles away. He connected his return unerringly with the web of trouble which had been weaving about him of late. He conceived himself to have been most unjustly spied upon and suspected, and was full of resentment at the conduct of Captain Chester. But Chester was an old granny, who sometimes made blunders and had to back down. It was a different thing when Armitage took hold. Jerrold looked sulkily into the clear, stern, blue eyes a moment, and the first impulse of rebellion wilted. He gave one irresolute glance around the quadrangle, then motioned with his hand to the open door. Something of the old, jaunty, Creole lightness of manner reasserted itself.

"After you, captain," he said.

XIII

Once within-doors, it was too dark for Armitage to see the features of his lieutenant; and he had his own reasons for desiring to read them. Mr. Jerrold, on the other hand, seemed disposed to keep in the shadows as much as possible. He made no movement to open the shutters of the one window which admitted light from the front, and walked back to his bedroom door, glanced in there as though to see that there were no occupants, then carefully closed it as he returned to face his captain. He took off his helmet and placed it on the centre-table, then, thrusting his thumbs inside the handsome, gold-broidered sword-belt, stood in a jaunty attitude but with a very uneasy look in his eyes to hear what his senior might have to say. Between the two men an invitation to sit would have been a superfluity. Neither had ever remained long enough in the other's quarters, since the exchange of the first calls when Jerrold came to the garrison, to render a chair at all necessary.

"Be good enough to strike a light, Mr. Jerrold," said Armitage, presently, seeing that his unwilling host made no effort on his own account.

"I proposed going out at once, captain, and presume you cannot have any very extended remarks to make."

"You cannot see the writing I have to call your attention to without a light. I shall detain you no longer than is necessary. Had you an engagement?"

"Nothing of great consequence. I presume it will keep."

"It will have to. The matter I have come upon will admit no further delay. Light your lamp, if you please."

And Jerrold did so, slowly and with much reluctance. He wiped his forehead vigorously the instant the flame began to splutter, but as the clear, steady light of the argand gradually spread over the little room Armitage could see the sweat again beading his forehead, and the dark eyes were glancing nervously about, and the hands that were so firm and steady and fine the year before and held the Springfield in so light yet immovable an aim were twitching now. It was no wonder Jerrold's score had dropped some thirty per cent. His nerve had gone to pieces.

Armitage stood and watched him a moment. Then he slowly spoke:

"I have no desire to allude to the subject of your conversation with Merrick. It was to put an end to such a thing—not to avail myself of any information it might give—that I hurried in. We will put that aside and go at once to the matter that brings me back. You are aware, of course, that your conduct has compromised a woman's name, and that the garrison is talking of nothing else."

Jerrold grasped the back of a chair with one slender brown hand, and looked furtively about as though for some hope of escape. Something like a startled gulp seemed to work his throat-muscles an instant; then he stammered his reply:

"I don't know what you mean."

"You *do* know what I mean. Captain Chester has already told you."

"Captain Chester came in here and made an unauthorized inspection of my quarters because he heard a shot fired by a sentry. I was out: I don't deny that. But he proceeded to say all manner of insulting and unwarrantable things, and tried to force me to hand in a resignation, simply because I was out of quarters after taps. I could account for *his* doing something so idiotic, but I'm at a loss to comprehend your taking it up."

"The most serious allegation ever made against an officer of the regiment is made against you, the senior lieutenant of my company, and the evidence furnished me by the colonel and by Captain Chester is of such a character that, unless you can refute it and clear her name, you will have a settlement with me to start with, and your dismissal from the regiment—"

"Settlement with you? What concern have you in the matter?" interrupted Jerrold.

"Waste no words on that, Mr. Jerrold. Understand that where her name is concerned no man on earth is more interested than I. Now answer me. You were absent from your quarters for some hours after the doctor's party. Somebody believed to have been you was seen and fired at for refusing to halt at the order of Captain Chester at 3.30 in the morning. The ladder that usually hung at your fence was found at the colonel's while you were out, and that night a woman's name was compromised beyond repair unless you can repair it. Unless you prove beyond peradventure where you were both that night and last night,—prove beyond question that you were not where you are believed to have been,—her name is stained and yours blackened forever. There are other things you must fully explain; but these first."

Jerrold's face was growing gray and sickly. He stared at the stern eyes before him, and could make no answer. His lips moved dryly, but made no sound.

"Come, I want to hear from you. Where were you, if not with, or seeking, her? Name your place and witnesses."

"By God, Captain Armitage, the army is no longer a place for a gentleman, if his every movement is to be spied upon like this!"

"The world is no place for a man of your stamp, is perhaps a better way of putting it," said Armitage, whose fingers were twitching convulsively, and whose whole frame quivered with the effort he was making to restrain the rage and indignation that consumed him. He could not—he would not—believe in her guilt. He must have this man's proof, no matter how it might damn *him* for good and all, no matter whom else it might involve, so long as it cleared her precious name. He must be patient, he must be calm and resolute; but the man's cold-blooded, selfish, criminal concealment nearly maddened him. With infinite effort he controlled himself, and went on:

"But it is of her I'm thinking, not of you. It is the name you have compromised and can clear, and should clear, even at the expense of your own,—in fact, Mr. Jerrold, *must* clear. Now will you tell me where you were and how you can prove it?"

"I decline to say. I won't be cross-questioned by men who have no authority. Captain Chester said he would refer it to the colonel; and when *he* asks I will answer,—not until then."

"I ask in his name. I am authorized by him, for he is not well enough to meet the ordeal."

"You say so, and I don't mean to dispute your word, Captain Armitage, but I have a right to demand some proof. How am I to know he authorized you?"

"He himself gave me this letter, in your handwriting," said Armitage; and, opening the long envelope, he held forth the missive over which the poor old colonel had gone nearly wild. "He found it the morning they left,—in her garden."

If Jerrold's face had been gray before, it was simply ghastly now. He recoiled from the sight after one fruitless effort to grasp the letter, then rallied with unlooked-for spirit:

"By heaven, Armitage, suppose I *did* write that letter? What does it prove but what I say,—that somebody has been prying and spying into my affairs? How came the colonel by it, if not by fraud or treachery?"

"He picked it up in the garden, I tell you,—among the rose-bushes, where she—where Miss Renwick had been but a few moments before, and where it might appear that she had dropped it."

"*She!* That letter! What had she to do with it? What right had she to read it?"

Armitage stepped impulsively forward. A glad, glorious light was bursting upon his soul. He could almost have seized Jerrold's hand and thanked him; but proofs—proofs were what he needed. It was not his mind that was to be convinced, it was "society" that must be satisfied of her utter innocence, that it might be enabled to say, "Well, I never for a moment believed a word of it." Link by link the chain of circumstantial evidence must be destroyed, and this was only one.

"You mean that that letter was not intended for Miss Renwick?" he asked, with eagerness he strove hard to repress.

"It was never meant for anybody," said Jerrold, the color coming back to his face and courage to his eyes. "That letter was never sent by me to any woman. It's my writing, of course, I can't deny that; but I never even meant it to go. If it left that desk it must have been stolen. I've been hunting high and low for it. I knew that such a thing lying around loose would be the cause of mischief. God! is *that* what all this fuss is about?" And he looked warily, yet with infinite anxiety, into his captain's eyes.

"There is far more to it, as you well know, sir," was the stern answer. "For whom was this written, if not for her? It won't do to *half* clear her name."

"Answer me this, Captain Armitage. Do you mean that that letter has compromised Miss Renwick?—that it is she whose name has been involved, and that it was of her that Chester meant to speak?"

"Certainly it was,—and I too."

There was an instant's silence; then Jerrold began to laugh nervously:

"Oh, well, I fancy it isn't the first time the revered and respected captain has got away off the track. All the same I do not mean to overlook his language to me; and I may say right now, Captain Armitage, that yours, too, calls for explanation."

"You shall have it in short order, Mr. Jerrold, and the sooner you understand the situation the better. So far as I am concerned, Miss Renwick needed no defender; but, thanks to your mysterious and unwarranted absence from quarters two very unlucky nights, and to other circumstances I have no need to name, and to your *penchant* for letter-writing of a most suggestive character, it *is* Miss Renwick whose name has been brought into question here at this post, and most prominently so. In plain words, Mr. Jerrold, you who brought this trouble upon her by your own misconduct must clear her, no matter at whose expense, or—"

"Or what?"

"I make no threats. I prefer that you should make the proper explanations from a proper sense of what is due."

"And suppose I say that no man is called upon to explain a situation which has been distorted and misrepresented by the evil imagination of his fellows?"

"Then I may have to wring the truth out of you,—and *will*; but, for her sake, I want as little publicity as possible. After this display on your part, I am not bound to show you any consideration whatever. Understand this, however: the array of evidence that you were feloniously inside Colonel Maynard's quarters that night and at his cottage window last night is of such a character that a court would convict you unless your *alibi* was conclusive. Leave the service you certainly shall, unless this whole thing is cleared up."

"I never was anywhere near Colonel Maynard's either last night or the other night I was absent."

"You will have to prove it. Mere denials won't help you in the face of such evidence as we have that you were there the first time."

"What evidence?"

"The photograph that was stolen from Mrs. Maynard between two and four o'clock that morning was seen in your drawer by Major Sloat at reveille. You were fool enough to show it to him."

"Captain Armitage, I shall be quite able to show, when the proper time comes, that the photograph I showed Major Sloat was *not* stolen: it was given me."

"That is beyond belief, Mr. Jerrold. Once and for all, understand this case. You have compromised her good name by the very mystery of your actions. You have it in your power to clear her by proving where you were, since you were not near her,—by showing how you got that photograph,—by explaining how you came to write so strange a letter. Now I say to you, will you do it, instantly, or must we wring it from you?"

A sneering smile was the only answer for a moment; then,—

"I shall take great pleasure in confounding my enemies should the matter be brought before a court,—I'm sure if the colonel can stand that sort of thing I can,—but as for defending myself or anybody else from utterly unjust and proofless suspicions, it's quite another thing."

"Good God, Jerrold! do you realize what a position you are taking? Do you—"

"Oh, not at all, captain," was the airy reply, "not at all. It is not a position I have taken: it is one into which you misguided conspirators have forced me. I certainly am not

Charles King

required to compromise anybody else in order to relieve a suspicion which you, not I, have created. How do you know that there may not be some other woman whose name I propose to guard? You have been really very flattering in your theories so far."

Armitage could bear no more. The airy conceit and insolence of the man overcame all self-restraint and resolution. With one bound he was at his throat, his strong white hands grasping him in a sudden, vice-like grip, then hurling him with stunning, thundering force to the floor. Down, headlong, went the tall lieutenant, his sword clattering by his side, his slim brown hands clutching wildly at anything that might bear him up, and dragging with him in his catastrophe a rack of hunting-pouches, antlers, and one heavy double-barrelled shot-gun. All came tumbling down about the struggling form, and Armitage, glaring down at him with clinching fists and rasping teeth, had only time to utter one deep-drawn malediction when he noted that the struggles ceased and Jerrold lay quite still. Then the blood began to ooze from a jagged cut near the temple, and it was evident that the hammer of the gun had struck him.

Another moment, and the door opened, and with anxious face Chester strode into the room. "You haven't killed him, Armitage? Is it as bad as that?"

"Pick him up, and we'll get him on the bed. He's only stunned. I didn't even hit him. Those things tumbled after-wards," said Armitage, as between them they raised the dead weight of the slender Adonis in their arms and bore him to the bedroom. Here they bathed the wound with cold water and removed the uniform coat, and presently the lieutenant began to revive and look about him.

"Who struck me?" he faintly asked.

"Your shot-gun fell on your head, but I threw you down, Jerrold. I'm sorry I touched you, but you're lucky it was no worse. This thing is going to raise a big bump here. Shall I send the doctor?"

"No. I'll come round presently. We'll see about this thing afterwards."

"Is there any friend you want to see? Shall I send word to anybody?" asked Chester.

"No. Don't let anybody come. Tell my striker to bring my breakfast; but I want nothing to-night but to be let alone."

"At least you will let me help you undress and get to bed?" said Chester.

"No. I wish you'd go,—both of you. I want quiet,—peace,— and there's none of it with either of you."

And so they left him. Later Captain Chester had gone to the quarters, and, after much parleying from without, had gained admission. Jerrold's head was bound in a bandage wet with arnica and water. He had been solacing himself with a pipe and a whiskey toddy, and was in a not unnaturally ugly mood.

"You may consider yourself excused from duty until your face is well again, by which time this matter will be decided. I admonish you to remain here and not leave the post until it is."

"You can prefer charges and see what you'll make of it," was the vehement reply. "Devil a bit will I help you out of the thing, after this night's work."

XIV

Tuesday, and the day of the long-projected german had come; and if ever a lot of garrison-people were wishing themselves well out of a flurry it was the social circle at Sibley. Invitations had been sent to all the prominent people in town who had shown any interest in the garrison since the regiment's arrival; beautiful favors had been procured; an elaborate supper had been prepared,—the ladies contributing their efforts to the salads and other solids, the officers wisely confining their donations to the wines. It was rumored that new and original figures were to be danced, and much had been said about this feature in town, and much speculation had been indulged in; but the Beaubien residence had been closed until the previous day, Nina was away with her mother and beyond reach of question, and Mr. Jerrold had not shown his face in town since her departure. Nor was he accessible when visitors inquired at the fort. They had never known such mysterious army people in their lives. What on earth could induce them to be so close-mouthed about a mere german? one might suppose they had something worth concealing; and presently it became noised abroad that there was genuine cause for perplexity, and possibly worse.

To begin with, every one at Sibley now knew something of the night adventure at the colonel's, and, as no one could give the true statement of the case, the stories in circulation were gorgeous embellishments of the actual facts. It would be useless, even if advisable, to attempt to reproduce these wild theories, but never was army garrison so tumultuously stirred by the whirlwind of rumor. It was no longer denied for an instant that the absence of the colonel and his household was the direct result of that night's discoveries; and when, to Mrs. Hoyt's inexpressible relief, there came a prettily-worded note from Alice on Monday evening informing her that neither the colonel nor her mother felt well enough to return to Sibley for the german, and that she herself preferred not to leave her mother at a time when she needed her care, Mrs. Hoyt and her intimates, with whom she instantly conferred, decided that there could be no doubt whatever that the colonel knew of the affair, had forbidden their return, and was only waiting for further evidence to decide what was to be done with his erring step-daughter. Women talked with bated breath of the latest stories in circulation, of Chester's moody silence and preoccupation, of Jerrold's ostracism, and of Frank Armitage's sudden return.

On Monday morning the captain had quietly appeared in uniform at the office, and it was known that he had relinquished the remainder of his leave of absence and resumed command of his company. There were men in the garrison who well knew that it was because of the mystery over-hanging the colonel's household that Armitage had so suddenly returned. They asked no questions and sought no explanation. All men marked, however, that Jerrold was not at the office on Monday, and many curiously looked at the morning report in the adjutant's office. No, he was not in arrest; neither was he on sick-report. He was marked present for duty, and yet he was not at the customary assembly of all the commissioned officers at head-quarters. More mystery, and most exasperating, too, it was known that Armitage and Jerrold had held a brief talk in the latter's quarters soon after Sunday's evening parade, and that the former had been reinforced for a time by Captain Chester, with whom he was afterwards closeted. Officers who heard that he had suddenly returned and was at Chester's went speedily to the latter's quarters,—at least two or three did,—and were met by a servant at the door, who said that the gentlemen had just gone out the back way. And, sure enough, neither Chester nor Armitage came home until long after taps; and then the colonel's cook told several people that the two gentlemen had spent over an hour up-stairs in the colonel's and Miss Alice's room and "was foolin' around the house till near ten o'clock."

Another thing that added to the flame of speculation and curiosity was this. Two of the ladies, returning from a moonlit stroll on the terrace just after tattoo, came through the narrow passage-way on the west side of the colonel's quarters, and there, at the foot of the little flight of steps leading up to the parade, they came suddenly upon Captain Chester, who was evidently only moderately pleased to see them and nervously anxious to expedite their onward movement. With the perversity of both sexes, however, they stopped to chat and inquire what he was doing there, and in the midst of it all a faint light gleamed on the opposite wall and the reflection of the curtains in Alice Renwick's window was distinctly visible. Then a sturdy masculine shadow appeared, and there was a rustling above, and then, with exasperating, mysterious, and epigrammatic terseness, a deep voice propounded the utterly senseless question,—

"How's that?"

To which, in great embarrassment, Chester replied,—

"Hold on a minute. I'm talking with some interested spectators."

Whereat the shadow of the big man shot out of sight, and the ladies found that it was useless to remain,—there would be no further developments so long as they did; and so they came away, with many a lingering backward look. "But the idea of asking such a fool question as 'How's that?' Why couldn't the man *say* what he meant?" It was gathered, however, that Armitage and Chester had been making some experiments that bore in some measure on the mystery. And all this time Mr. Jerrold was in his quarters, only a stone's-throw away. How interested *he* must have been!

But, while the garrison was relieved at knowing that Alice Renwick would not be on hand for the german and it was being fondly hoped she might never return to the post, there was still another grievous embarrassment. How about Mr. Jerrold?

He had been asked to lead when the german was first projected, and had accepted. That was fully two weeks before; and now—no one knew just what ought to be done. It was known that Nina Beaubien had returned on the previous day from a brief visit to the upper lakes, and that she had a costume of ravishing beauty in which to carry desolation to the hearts of the garrison belles in leading that german with Mr. Jerrold. Old Madame Beaubien had been reluctant, said her city friends, to return at all. She heartily disapproved of Mr. Jerrold, and was bitterly set against Nina's growing infatuation for him. But Nina was headstrong and deter-mined: moreover, she was far more than a match for her mother's vigilance, and it was known at Sibley that two or three times the girl had been out at the fort with the Suttons and other friends when the old lady believed her in quarters totally different. Cub Sutton had confided to Captain Wilton that Madame Beaubien was in total ignorance of the fact that there was to be a party at the doctor's the night he had driven out with Nina and his sister, and that Nina had "pulled the wool over her mother's eyes" and made her believe she was going to spend the evening with friends in town, naming a family with whom the Beaubiens were intimate. A long drive always made the old lady sleepy, and, as she had accompanied Nina to the fort that afternoon, she went early to bed, having secured her wild birdling, as she supposed, from possibility of further meetings with Jerrold. For nearly a week, said Cub, Madame Beaubien had dogged Nina so that she could not get a moment with the man with whom she was evidently so smitten, and the girl was almost at her wits' end with seeing the depth of his flirtation with Alice Renwick and the knowledge that on the morrow her mother would spirit her off to the cool breezes and blue waves of the great lake. Cub said she so worked on Fanny's feelings that they put up the scheme together and made him bring them out. Gad! if old Maman only found it out there'd be no more germans for Nina. She'd ship her off to the good Sisters at Creve-Coeur and slap her into a convent and leave all her money to the Church.

And yet, said city society, old Maman idolized her beautiful daughter and could deny her no luxury or indulgence. She dressed her superbly, though with a somewhat barbaric taste where Nina's own good sense and Eastern teaching did not interfere. What she feared was that the girl would fall in love with some adventurer, or—what was quite as bad—some army man who would carry her darling away to Arizona or other inaccessible spot. Her plan was that Nina should marry here—at home—some one of the staid young merchant princes rising into prominence in the Western metropolis, and from the very outset Nina had shown a singular infatuation for the buttons and straps and music and heaven-knows-what-all out at the fort. She gloried in seeing her daughter prominent in all scenes of social life. She rejoiced in her triumphs, and took infinite pains with all preparations. She would have set her foot against Nina's simply dancing the german at the fort with Jerrold as a partner, but she could not resist it that the papers should announce on Sunday morning that "the event of the season at Fort Sibley was the german given last Tuesday night by the ladies of the garrison and led by the lovely Miss Beaubien" with Lieutenant or Captain Anybody. There were a dozen bright, graceful, winning women among the dames and damsels at the fort, and Alice Renwick was a famous beauty by this time. It was more than Maman Beaubien could withstand, that her Nina should "lead" all these, and so her consent was won. Back they came from Chequamegon, and the stately home on Summit Avenue reopened to receive them. It was Monday noon when they returned, and by three o'clock Fanny Sutton had told Nina Beaubien what she knew of the wonderful rumors that were floating in from Sibley. She was more than half disposed to be in love with Jerrold herself. She expected a proper amount of womanly horror, incredulity, and indignation; but she was totally unprepared for the outburst that followed. Nina was transformed into a tragedy queen on the instant, and poor, simple-hearted, foolish Fanny Sutton was almost scared out of her small wits by the fire of denunciation and fury with which her story was greeted. She came home with white, frightened face and hunted up Cub and told him that she had been telling Nina some of the queer things the ladies had been saying about Mr. Jerrold, and Nina almost tore her to pieces, and could he go right out to the fort to see Mr. Jerrold? Nina wanted to send a note at once; and if he couldn't go she had made her promise that she would get somebody to go instantly and to come back and let her know before four o'clock. Cub was always glad of an excuse to go out to the fort, but a coldness had sprung up between him and Jerrold. He had heard the ugly rumors in that mysterious way in which all such things are heard, and, while his shallow pate could not quite conceive of such a monstrous scandal and he did not believe half he heard, he sagely felt that in the presence of so much smoke there was surely some fire, and avoided the man from whom he had been inseparable. Of course he had not spoken to him on the subject, and, singularly enough, this was the case with all the officers at the post except Armitage and the commander. It was understood that the matter was in Chester's hands, to do with as was deemed best. It was believed that his resignation had been tendered; and all these forty-eight hours since the story might be said to be fairly before the public, Jerrold had been left much to himself, and was presumably in the depths of dismay.

One or two men, urged by their wives, who thought it was really time something were done to let him understand he ought not to lead the german, had gone to see him and been refused admission. Asked from within what they wanted, the reply was somewhat difficult to frame, and in both cases resolved itself into "Oh, about the german;" to which Jerrold's voice was heard to say, "The german's all right. I'll lead if I'm well enough and am not bothered to death meantime; but I've got some private matters to attend to, and am not seeing anybody to-day." And with this answer they were fain to be content. It had been settled, however, that the officers were to tell Captain Chester at ten o'clock that in their opinion Mr. Jerrold ought not to be permitted to attend so long as this mysterious charge hung over him; and Mr. Rollins had been notified that he must be ready to lead.

Poor Rollins! He was in sore perplexity. He wanted nothing better than to dance with Nina Beaubien. He wondered if she *would* lead with him, or would even come at all when she learned that Jerrold would be unable to attend. "Sickness" was to be the ostensible cause, and in the youth and innocence of his heart Rollins never supposed that Nina would hear of all the other assignable reasons. He meant to ride in and call upon her Monday evening; but, as ill luck would have it, old Sloat, who was officer of the day, stepped on a round pebble as he was going down the long flight to the railway-station, and sprained his ankle. Just at five o'clock Rollins got orders to relieve him, and was returning from the guard-house, when who should come driving in but Cub Sutton, and Cub reined up and asked where he would be apt to find Mr. Jerrold.

"He isn't well, and has been denying himself to all callers to-day," said Rollins, shortly.

"Well, I've got to see him, or at least get a note to him," said Cub. "It's from Miss Beaubien, and requires an answer."

"You know the way to his quarters, I presume," said Rollins, coldly: "you have been there frequently. I will have a man hold your horse, or you can tie him there at the rail, just as you please."

"Thanks. I'll go over, I believe." And go he did, and poor Rollins was unable to resist the temptation of watching whether the magic name of Nina would open the door. It did not; but he saw Cub hand in the little note through the shutters, and ere long there came another from within. This Cub stowed in his waistcoat-pocket and drove off with, and Rollins walked jealously homeward. But that evening he went through a worse experience, and it was the last blow to his budding passion for sparkling-eyed Nina.

It was nearly tattoo, and a dark night, when Chester suddenly came in:

"Rollins, you remember my telling you I was sure some of the men had been getting liquor in from the shore down below the station and 'running it' that way? I believe we can nab the smuggler this evening. There's a boat down there now. The corporal has just told me."

Smuggling liquor was one of Chester's horrors. He surrounded the post with a cordon of sentries who had no higher duty, apparently, than that of preventing the entrance of alcohol in any form. He had run a "red-cross" crusade against the post-trader's store in the matter of light wines and small beer, claiming that only adulterated stuff was sold to the men, and forbidding the sale of anything stronger than "pop" over the trader's counter. Then, when it became apparent that liquor was being brought on the reservation, he made vigorous efforts to break up the practice. Colonel Maynard rather poohpoohed the whole business. It was his theory that a man who was determined to have a drink might better be allowed to take an honest one, *coram publico*, than a smuggled and deleterious article; but he succumbed to the rule that only "light wines and beer" should be sold at the store, and was lenient to the poor devils who overloaded and deranged their stomachs in consequence. But Chester no sooner found himself in command than he launched into the crusade with redoubled energy, and spent hours of the day and night trying to capture invaders of the reservation with a bottle in their pockets. The bridge was guarded, so was the crossing of the Cloudwater to the south, and so were the two roads entering from the north and west; and yet there was liquor coming in, and, as though "to give Chester a benefit," some of the men in barracks had a royal old spree on Saturday night, and the captain was sorer-headed than any of the participants in consequence. In some way he heard that a rowboat came up at night and landed supplies of contraband down by the river-side out of sight and hearing of the sentry at the railway-station, and it was thither he hurriedly led Rollins this Monday evening.

They turned across the railway on reaching the bottom of the long stairs, and scrambled down the rocky embankment on the other side, Rollins following in reluctant silence and holding his sword so that it would not rattle, but he had no faith in the theory of smugglers. He felt in some vague and unsatisfactory way a sense of discomfort and anxiety over his captain's late proceedings, and this stealthy descent seemed fraught with ill omen.

Once down in the flats, their footsteps made no noise in the yielding sand, and all was silence save for the plash of the waters along the shores. Far down the river were the reflections of one or two twinkling lights, and close under the bank in the slack-water a few stars were peeping at their own images, but no boat was there, and the captain led still farther to a little copse of willow, and there, in the shadows, sure enough, was a row-boat, with a little lantern dimly burning, half hidden in the stern.

Not only that, but as they halted at the edge of the willows the captain put forth a warning hand and cautioned silence. No need. Rollins's straining eyes were already fixed on two figures that were standing in the shadows not ten feet away,—one that of a tall, slender man, the other a young girl. It was a moment before Rollins could recognize either; but in that moment the girl had turned suddenly, had thrown her arms about the neck of the tall young man, and, with her head pillowed on his breast, was gazing up in his face.

"Kiss me once more, Howard. Then I must go," they heard her whisper.

Rollins seized his captain's sleeve, and strove, sick at heart, to pull him back; but Chester stoutly stood his ground. In the few seconds more that they remained they saw his arms more closely enfold her. They saw her turn at the brink, and, in an utter abandonment of rapturous, passionate love, throw her arms again about his neck and stand on tiptoe to reach his face with her warm lips. They could not fail to hear the caressing tone of her every word, or to mark his receptive but gloomy silence. They could not mistake the voice,—the form, shadowy though it was. The girl was Nina Beaubien, and the man, beyond question, Howard Jerrold. They saw him hand her into the light skiff and hurriedly kiss her good-night. Once again, as though she could not leave him, her arms were thrown about his neck and she clung to him with all her strength; then the little boat swung slowly out into the stream, the sculls were shipped, and with practised hand Nina Beaubien pulled forth into the swirling waters of the river, and the faint light, like slowly-setting star, floated downward with the sweeping tide and finally disappeared beyond the point.

Then Jerrold turned to leave, and Chester stepped forth and confronted him:

"Mr. Jerrold, did I not instruct you to confine yourself to your quarters until satisfactory explanation was made of the absences with which you are charged?"

Jerrold started at the abrupt and unlooked-for greeting, but his answer was prompt:

"Not at all, sir. You gave me to understand that I was to remain here—not to leave the post—until you had decided on certain points; and, though I do not admit the justice of your course, and though you have put me to grave inconvenience, I obeyed the order. I needed to go to town to-day on urgent business, but, between you and Captain Armitage, am in no condition to go. For all this, sir, there will come proper retribution when my colonel returns. And now, sir, you are spying upon me,—*spying*, I say,—and it only confirms what I said of you before."

"Silence, Mr. Jerrold! This is insubordination."

"I don't care a damn what it is, sir! There is nothing contemptuous enough for me to say of you or your conduct to me—"

"Not another word, Mr. Jerrold! Go to your quarters in arrest.—Mr. Rollins, you are witness to this language."

But Rollins was not. Turning from the spot in blankness of heart before a word was uttered between them, he followed the waning light with eyes full of yearning and trouble; he trudged his way down along the sandy shore until he came to the silent waters of the slough and could go no farther; and then he sat him down and covered his face with his hands. It was pretty hard to bear.

XV

Tuesday still, and all manner of things had happened and were still to happen in the hurrying hours that followed Sunday night. The garrison woke at Tuesday's reveille in much perturbation of spirit, as has been said, but by eight o'clock and breakfast-time one cause of perplexity was at an end. Relief had come with Monday afternoon and Alice Renwick's letter saying she would not attend the german, and now still greater relief in the news that sped from mouth to mouth: Lieutenant Jerrold was in close arrest. Armitage and Chester had been again in consultation Monday night, said the gossips, and something new had been discovered,—no one knew just what,—and the toils had settled upon Jerrold's handsome head, and now he was to be tried. As usual in such cases, the news came in through the kitchen, and most officers heard it at the breakfast-table from the lips of their better halves, who could hardly find words to express their sentiments as to the inability of their lords to explain the new phase of the situation. When the first sergeant of Company B came around to Captain Armitage with the sick-book, soon after six in the morning, the captain briefly directed him to transfer Lieutenant Jerrold on the morning report from present for duty to "in arrest," and no sooner was it known at the quarters of Company B than it began to work back to Officers' Row through the medium of the servants and strikers.

It was the sole topic of talk for a full hour. Many ladies who had intended going to town by the early train almost perilled their chances of catching the same in their eagerness to hear further details.

But the shriek of the whistle far up the valley broke up the group that was so busily chatting and speculating over in the quadrangle, and, with shy yet curious eyes, the party of at least a dozen—matrons and maids, wives or sisters of the officers—scurried past the darkened windows of Mr. Jerrold's quarters, and through the mysterious passage west of the colonel's silent house, and down the long stairs, just in time to catch the train that whirled them away city-ward almost as soon as it had disgorged the morning's mail. Chatting and laughing, and full of blithe anticipation of the glories of the coming german, in preparation for which most of their number had found it necessary to run in for just an hour's shopping, they went jubilantly on their way. Shopping done, they would all meet, take luncheon together at the "Woman's Exchange," return to the post by the afternoon train, and have plenty of time for a little nap before dressing for the german. Perhaps the most interesting question now up for discussion was, who would lead with Mr. Rollins? The train went puffing into the crowded depot: the ladies hastened forth, and in a moment were on the street; cabs and carriages were passed in disdain; a brisk walk of a block carried them to the main thoroughfare and into the heart of the shopping district; a rush of hoofs and wheels and pedestrians there encountered them, and the roar assailed their sensitive and unaccustomed ears, yet high above it all pierced and pealed the shrill voices of the newsboys darting here and there with their eagerly-bought journals. But women bent on germans and shopping have time and ears for no such news as that which demands the publication of extras. Some of them never hear or heed the cry, "Indian Massacree!" "Here y'are! All about the killin' of Major

Thornton an' his sojers!" "Extry!—extry!" It is not until they reach the broad portals of the great Stewart of the West that one of their number, half incredulously, buys a copy and reads aloud: "Major Thornton,—th Infantry, Captain Langham and Lieutenant Bliss,—th Cavalry, and thirty men, are killed. Captains Wright and Lane and Lieutenants Willard and Brooks,—th Cavalry, and some forty more men, are seriously wounded. The rest of the command is corralled by an overwhelming force of Indians, and their only hope is to hold out until help can reach them. All troops along the line of the Union Pacific are already under orders."

"Oh, isn't it dreadful?"

"Yes; but aren't you glad it wasn't Ours? Oh, look! there's Nina Beaubien over there in her carriage. *Do* let's find out if she's going to lead with Rollins!"

Vae victis! Far out in the glorious Park country in the heart of the Centennial State a little band of blue-coats, sent to succor a perilled agent, is making desperate stand against fearful odds. Less than two hundred men has the wisdom of the Department sent forth through the wilderness to find and, if need be, fight its way through five times its weight in well-armed foes. The officers and men have no special quarrel with those Indians, nor the Indians with them. Only two winters before, when those same Indians were sick and starving, and their lying go-betweens, the Bureau-employees, would give them neither food nor justice, a small band made their way to the railway and were fed on soldier food and their wrongs righted by soldier justice. But another snarl has come now, and this time the Bureau-people are in a pickle, and the army—ever between two fires at least, and thankful when it isn't six—is ordered to send a little force and go out there and help the agent maintain his authority. The very night before the column reaches the borders of the reservation the leading chiefs come in camp to interview the officers, shake hands, beg tobacco, and try on their clothes, then go back to their braves and laugh as they tell there are only a handful, and plan the morrow's ambuscade and massacre. *Vae victis*! There are women and children among the garrisons along the Union Pacific whose hearts have little room for thoughts of germans in the horror of this morning's tidings. But Sibley is miles and miles away, and, as Mrs. Wheeler says, aren't you glad it wasn't Ours?

Out at the fort there is a different scene. The morning journals and the clicking telegraph send a thrill throughout the whole command. The train has barely whistled out of sight when the ringing notes of officers' call resound through the quadrangle and out over the broader drill-ground beyond. Wondering, but prompt, the staid captains and eager subalterns come hurrying to head-quarters, and the band, that had come forth and taken its station on the parade, all ready for guard-mount, goes quickly back, while the men gather in big squads along the shaded row of their quarters and watch the rapid assembly at the office. And there old Chester, with kindling eyes, reads to the silent company the brief official order. Ay, though it be miles and miles away, fast as steam and wheel can take it, the good old regiment in all its sturdy strength goes forth to join the rescue of the imprisoned comrades far in the Colorado Rockies. "Have your entire command in readiness for immediate field-service in the Department of the Platte. Special train will be there to take you by noon at latest." And though many a man has lost friend and comrade in the tragedy that calls them forth, and though many a brow clouds for the moment with the bitter news of such useless sacrifice, every eye brightens, every muscle seems to brace, every nerve and pulse to throb and thrill with the glorious excitement of quick assembly and coming action. Ay, we are miles and miles away; we leave the dear old post, with homes and firesides, wives, children, and sweethearts, all to the care of the few whom sickness or old wounds or advancing years render unfit for hard, sharp marching; and, thank God! we'll be there to take a hand and help those gallant fellows out of their "corral" or to have one good blow at the cowardly hounds who lured and lied to them.

How the "assembly" rings on the morning air! How quick they spring to ranks, those eager bearded faces and trim blue-clad forms! How buoyant and brisk even the elders seem as the captains speed over to their company quarters and the quick, stirring orders are given! "Field kits; all the cooked rations you have on hand; overcoat, blanket, extra socks and underclothes; every cartridge you've got; haversack and canteen, and nothing else. Now get ready,—lively!" How irrepressible is the cheer that goes up! How we pity the swells of the light battery who have to stay! How wistful those fellows look, and how eagerly they throng about the barracks, yearning to go, and, since that is denied, praying to be of use in some way! Small wonder is it that all the bustle and excitement penetrates the portals of Mr. Jerrold's darkened quarters, and the shutters are thrown open and his bandaged head comes forth.

"What is it, Harris?" he demands of a light-batteryman who is hurrying past.

"Orders for Colorado, sir. The regiment goes by special train. Major Thornton's command's been massacred, and there's a big fight ahead."

"My God! Here!—stop one moment. Run over to Company B and see if you can find my servant, or Merrick, or somebody. If not, you come back quick. I want to send a note to Captain Armitage."

"I can take it, sir. We're not going. The band and the battery have to stay."

And Jerrold, with trembling hand and feverish haste, seats himself at the same desk whence on that fatal morning he sent the note that wrought such disaster; and as he rises and hands his missive forth, throwing wide open the shutters as he does so, his bedroom doors fly open, and a whirling gust of the morning wind sweeps through from rear to front, and half a score of bills and billets, letters and scraps of paper, go ballooning out upon the parade.

"By heaven!" he mutters, "that's how it happened, is it? *Look* at them go!" for going they were, in spiral eddies or fluttering skips, up the grassy "quad," and over among the rose-bushes of Alice Renwick's garden. Over on the other side of the narrow, old-fashioned frontier fort the men were bustling about, and their exultant, eager voices rang out on the morning air. All was life and animation, and even in Jerrold's selfish soul there rose responsive echo to the soldierly spirit that seemed to pervade the whole command. It was their first summons to active field-duty with prospective battle since he had joined, and, with all his shortcomings as a "duty" officer in garrison and his many frailties of character, Jerrold was not the man to lurk in the rear when there was danger ahead. It dawned on him with sudden and crushing force that now it lay in the power of his enemies to do him vital injury,—that he could be held here at the post like a suspected felon, a mark for every finger, a target for every tongue, while every other officer of his regiment was hurrying with his men to take his knightly share in the coming onset. It was intolerable, shameful. He paced the floor of his little parlor in nervous misery, ever and anon gazing from the window for sight of his captain. It was to him he had written, urging that he be permitted a few moments' talk. "This is no time for a personal misunderstanding," he wrote. "I must see you at once. I can clear away the doubts, can explain my action; but, for heaven's sake, intercede for me with Captain Chester that I may go with the command."

As luck would have it, Armitage was with Chester at the office when the letter was handed in. He opened it, gave a whistle of surprise, and simply held it forth to the temporary commander.

"Read that," he said.

Chester frowned, but took the note and looked it curiously over.

"I have no patience with the man now," he said. "Of course after what I saw last night I begin to understand the nature of his defence; but we don't want any such man in the regiment, after this. What's the use of taking him with us?"

"That isn't the point," said Armitage. "Now or never, possibly, is the time to clear up this mystery. Of course Maynard will be up to join us by the first train; and what won't it be worth to him to have positive proof that all his fears were unfounded?"

"Even if it wasn't Jerrold, there is still the fact that I saw a man clambering out of her window. How is that to be cleared up?" said Chester, gloomily.

"That may come later, and won't be such a bugbear as you think. If you were not worried into a morbid condition over all this trouble, you would not look so seriously upon a thing which I regard as a piece of mere night prowling, with a possible spice of romance."

"What romance, I'd like to know?"

"Never mind that now: I'm playing detective for the time being. Let me see Jerrold for you and find out what he has to offer. Then you can decide. Are you willing? All right! But remember this while I think of it. You admit that the light you saw on the wall Sunday night was exactly like that which you saw the night of your adventure, and that the shadows were thrown in the same way. You thought that night that the light was turned up and afterwards turned out in her room, and that it was *her* figure you saw at the window. Didn't you?"

"Yes. What then?"

"Well, I believe her statement that she saw and heard nothing until reveille. I believe it was Mrs. Maynard who did the whole thing, without Miss Renwick's knowing anything about it."

"Why?"

"Because I accomplished the feat with the aid of the little night-lamp that I found by the colonel's bedside. It is my theory that Mrs. Maynard was restless after the colonel finally fell asleep, that she heard your tumble, and took her little lamp, crossed over into Miss Renwick's room, opened the door without creaking, as I can do to your satisfaction, found her sleeping quietly, but the room a trifle close and warm, set her night-lamp down on the table, as I did, threw her shadow on the wall, as I did, and opened the shade, as you thought her daughter did. Then she withdrew, and left those doors open,—both hers and her daughter's,—and the light, instead of being turned down, as you thought, was simply carried back into her own room."

"That is all possible. But how about the man in her room? Nothing was stolen, though money and jewelry were lying around loose. If theft was not the object, what was?"

"Theft certainly was not, and I'm not prepared to say what was, but I have reason to believe it wasn't Miss Renwick."

"Anything to prove it?"

"Yes; and, though time is precious and I cannot show you, you may take my word for it. We must be off at noon, and both of us have much to do, but there may be no other chance to talk, and before you leave this post I want you to realize her utter innocence."

"I want to, Armitage."

"I know you do: so look here. We assume that the same man paid the night visit both here and at Sablon, and that he wanted to see the same person,—if he did not come to steal: do we not?"

"Yes."

"We know that at Sablon it was Mrs. Maynard he sought and called. The colonel says so."

"Yes."

"Presumably, then, it was she—not her daughter—he had some reasons for wanting to see here at Sibley. What is more, if he wanted to see Miss Renwick there was nothing to prevent his going right into her window?"

"Nothing."

"Well, I believe I can prove he didn't; on the contrary, that he went around by the roof of the porch to the colonel's room and tried there, but found it risky on account of the blinds, and that finally he entered the hall window,—what might be called neutral ground. The painters had been at work there, as you said, two days before, and the paint on the slats was not quite dry. The blinds and sills were the only things they had touched up on that front, it seems, and nothing on the sides. Now, on the fresh paint of the colonel's slats are the new imprints of masculine thumb and fingers, and on the sill of the hall window is a footprint that I know to be other than Jerrold's."

"Why?"

"Because he doesn't own such a thing as this track was made with, and I don't know a man in this command who does. It was the handiwork of the Tonto Apaches, and came from the other side of the continent."

"You mean it was—?"

"Exactly. An Indian moccasin."

Meantime, Mr. Jerrold had been making hurried preparations, as he had fully determined that at any cost he would go with the regiment. He had been burning a number of letters, when Captain Armitage knocked and hurriedly entered. Jerrold pushed forward a chair and plunged at once into the matter at issue:

"There is no time to waste, captain. I have sent to you to ask what I can do to be released from arrest and permitted to go with the command."

"Answer the questions I put to you the other night, and

certify to your answers; and of course you'll have to apologize to Captain Chester for your last night's language."

"That of course; though you will admit it looked like spying. Now let me ask you, did he tell you who the lady was?"

"No. I told him."

"How did you know?"

"By intuition, and my knowledge of previous circumstances."

"We have no time to discuss it. I make no attempt to conceal it now; but I ask that, on your honor, neither you nor he reveal it."

"And continue to let the garrison believe that you were in Miss Renwick's room that ghastly night?" asked Armitage, dryly.

Jerrold flushed: "I have denied that, and I would have proved my *alibi* could I have done so without betraying a woman's secret. Must I tell?"

"So far as I am concerned, Mr. Jerrold," said Armitage, with cold and relentless meaning, "you not only must tell—you must *prove*—both that night's doings and Saturday night's,— both that and how you obtained that photograph."

"My God! In one case it is a woman's name; in the other I have promised on honor not to reveal it."

"That ends it, then. You remain here in close arrest, and the charges against you will be pushed to the bitter end. I will write them this very hour."

XVI

At ten o'clock that morning, shortly after a smiling interview with the ladies of Fort Sibley, in which, with infinite spirit and the most perfect self-control, Miss Beaubien had informed them that she had promised to lead with Mr. Jerrold, and, since he was in duress, she would lead with no one, and sent them off wondering and greatly excited, there came running up to the carriage a telegraph messenger boy, who handed her a despatch.

"I was going up to the avenue, mum," he explained, "but I seen you here."

Nina's face paled as she tore it open and read the curt lines:

"Come to me, here. Your help needed instantly."

She sprang from the carriage. "Tell mother I have gone over to see some Fort friends,—not to wait," she called to the coachman, well knowing he would understand that she meant the ladies with whom she had been so recently talking. Like a frightened deer she sped around the corner, hailed the driver of a cab, lounging with his fellows along the walk, ordered him to drive with all speed to Summit Avenue, and with beating heart decided on her plan. Her glorious eyes were flashing: the native courage and fierce determination of

her race were working in her woman's heart. She well knew
that imminent danger threatened him. She had dared
everything for love of his mere presence, his sweet caress.
What would she not dare to save him, if save she could? He
had not been true to her. She knew, and knew well, that,
whether sought or not, Alice Renwick had been winning him
from her, that he was wavering, that he had been cold and
negligent; but with all her soul and strength she loved him,
and believed him grand and brave and fine as he was
beautiful. Now—now was her opportunity. He needed her.
His commission, his honor, depended on her. He had
intimated as much the night before,—had told her of the
accusations and suspicions that attached to him,—but made
no mention of the photograph. He had said that though
nothing could drag from him a word that would compromise
her, she might be called upon to stand 'twixt him and ruin;
and now perhaps the hour had come. She could free,
exonerate, glorify him, and in doing so claim him for her
own. Who, after this, could stand 'twixt her and him? He
loved her, though he *had* been cold; and she—? Had he
bidden her bow her dusky head to earth and kiss the print of
his heel, she would have obeyed could she but feel sure that
her reward would be a simple touch of his hand, an
assurance that no other woman could find a moment's place
in his love. Verily, he had been doing desperate wooing in
the long winter, for the very depths of her nature were all
athrob with love for him. And now he could no longer plead
that poverty withheld his offer of his hand. She would soon
be mistress of her own little fortune, and, at her mother's
death, of an independence. Go to him she would, and on
wings of the wind, and go she did. The cab released her at
the gate to her home, and went back with a double fare that
set the driver to thinking. She sped through the house, and
out the rear doors, much to the amaze of cook and others
who were in consultation in the kitchen. She flew down a
winding flight of stairs to the level below, and her fairy feet

went tripping over the pavement of a plebeian street. A quick turn, and she was at a little second-rate stable, whose proprietor knew her and started from his chair.

"What's wrong to-day, Miss Nina?"

"I want the roan mare and light buggy again,—quick as you can. Your own price at the old terms, Mr. Graves,— silence."

He nodded, called to a subordinate, and in five minutes handed her into the frail vehicle. An impatient chirrup and flap of the reins, and the roan shot forth into the dusty road, leaving old Graves shaking his head at the door.

"I've known her ever since she was weaned," he muttered, "and she's a wild bird, if ever there was one, but she's never been the like o' this till last month."

And the roan mare was covered with foam and sweat when Nina Beaubien drove into the bustling fort, barely an hour after her receipt of Jerrold's telegram. A few officers were gathered in front of head-quarters, and there were curious looks from face to face as she was recognized. Mr. Rollins was on the walk, giving some instructions to a sergeant of his company, and never saw her until the buggy reined up close behind him and, turning suddenly, he met her face to face as she sprang lightly to the ground. The young fellow reddened to his eyes, and would have recoiled, but she was mistress of the situation. She well knew she had but to command and he would obey, or, at the most, if she could no longer command she had only to implore, and he would be powerless to withstand her entreaty.

"I am glad *you* are here, Mr. Rollins. You can help me.— Sergeant, will you kindly hitch my horse at that post?—

Now," she added, in low, hurried tone, "come with me to Mr. Jerrold's."

Rollins was too stupefied to answer. Silently he placed himself by her side, and together they passed the group at the office. Miss Beaubien nodded with something of her old archness and coquetry to the cap-raising party, but never hesitated. Together they passed along the narrow board walk, followed by curious eyes, and as they reached the angle and stepped beneath the shelter of the piazza in front of the long, low, green-blinded Bachelors' Row, there was sudden sensation in the group. Mr. Jerrold appeared at the door of his quarters; Rollins halted some fifty feet away, raised his cap, and left her; and, all alone, with the eyes of Fort Sibley upon her, Nina Beaubien stepped bravely forward to meet her lover.

They saw him greet her at the door. Some of them turned away, unwilling to look, and yet unwilling to go and not understand this new phase of the mystery. Rollins, looking neither to right nor left, repassed them and walked off with a set, savage look on his young face, and then, as one or two still gazed, fascinated by this strange and daring proceeding, others, too, turned back and, half ashamed of themselves for such a yielding to curiosity, glanced furtively over at Jerrold's door.

There they stood,—he, restrained by his arrest, unable to come forth; she, restrained more by his barring form than by any consideration of maidenly reserve, for, had he bidden, she would have gone within. She had fully made up her mind that wherever he was, even were it behind the sentinels and bars of the guard-house, she would demand that she be taken to his side. He had handed out a chair, but she would not sit. They saw her looking up into his face as he talked, and noted the eager gesticulation, so characteristic of his Creole blood, that seemed to accompany his rapid words. They saw her bending towards him, looking eagerly up in his eyes, and occasionally casting indignant glances over towards the group at the office, as though she would annihilate with her wrath the persecutors of her hero. Then they saw her stretch forth both her hands with a quick impulsive movement, and grasp his one instant, looking so faithfully, steadfastly, loyally, into his clouded and anxious face. Then she turned, and with quick, eager steps came tripping towards them. They stood irresolute. Every man felt that it was somebody's duty to step forward, meet her, and be her escort though the party, but no one advanced. There was, if anything, a tendency to sidle towards the office door, as though to leave the sidewalk unimpeded. But she never sought to pass them by. With flashing eyes and crimson cheeks, she bore straight upon them, and, with indignant emphasis upon every word, accosted them:

"Captain Wilton, Major Sloat, I wish to see Captain Chester at once. Is he in the office?"

"Certainly, Miss Beaubien. Shall I call him? or will you walk in?" And both men were at her side in a moment.

"Thanks. I will go right in,—if you will kindly show me to him."

Another moment, and Armitage and Chester, deep in the midst of their duties and surrounded by clerks and orderlies and assailed by half a dozen questions in one and the same instant, looked up astonished as Wilton stepped in and announced Miss Beaubien desiring to see Captain Chester on immediate business. There was no time for conference. There she stood in the door-way, and all tongues were hushed on the instant. Chester rose and stepped forward with anxious courtesy. She did not choose to see the extended hand.

"It is you, alone, I wish to see, captain. Is it impossible here?"

"I fear it is, Miss Beaubien; but we can walk out in the open air. I feel that I know what it is you wish to say to me," he added, in a low tone, took his cap from the peg on which it hung, and led the way. Again she passed through the curious, but respectful group, and Jerrold, watching furtively from his window, saw them come forth.

The captain turned to her as soon as they were out of earshot:

"I have no daughter of my own, my dear young lady, but if I had I could not more thoroughly feel for you than I do. How can I help you?"

The reply was unexpectedly spirited. He had thought to encourage and sustain her, be sympathetic and paternal, but, as he afterwards ruefully admitted, he "never did seem to get the hang of a woman's temperament." Apparently sympathy was not the thing she needed.

"It is late in the day to ask such a question, Captain Chester. You have done great wrong and injustice. The question is now, will you undo it?"

He was too surprised to speak for a moment. When his tongue was unloosed he said,—

"I shall be glad to be convinced I was wrong."

"I know little of army justice or army laws, Captain Chester, but when a girl is compelled to take this step to rescue a friend there is something brutal about them,—or the men who enforce them. Mr. Jerrold tells me that he is arrested. I knew that last night, but not until this morning did he consent to let me know that he would be court-martialled unless he could prove where he was the night you were officer of the day two weeks ago, and last Saturday night. He is too noble and good to defend himself when by doing so he might harm me. But I am here to free him from the cruel suspicion you have formed." She had quickened her step, and in her impulsiveness and agitation they were almost at the end of the walk. He hesitated, as though reluctant to go along under the piazza, but she was imperious, and he yielded. "No, come!" she said. "I mean that you shall hear the whole truth, and that at once. I do not expect you to understand or condone my conduct, but you must acquit him. We are engaged; and—I love him. He has enemies here, as I see all too plainly, and they have prejudiced mother against him, and she has forbidden my seeing him. I came out to the fort without her knowledge one day, and it angered her. From that time she would not let me see him alone. She watched every movement, and came with me wherever I drove. She gave orders that I should never have any of our horses to drive or ride alone,—I, whom father had indulged to the utmost and who had ridden and driven at will from my babyhood. She came out to the fort with me that evening for parade, and never even agreed to let me go out to see some neighbors until she learned he was to escort Miss Renwick. She had ordered me to be ready to go with her to Chequamagon the next day, and I would not go until I had seen him. There had been a misunderstanding. I got the Suttons to drive me out while mother supposed me at the Laurents', and Mr. Jerrold promised to meet me east of the bridge and drive in town with us, and I was to send him back in Graves's buggy. He had been refused permission to leave the post, he said, and could not cross the bridge, where the sentries would be sure to recognize him, but, as it was our last chance of meeting, he risked the discovery of his absence, never dreaming of such a thing as his private rooms being inspected. He had a little skiff down in the willows that he had used before, and by leaving the party at midnight he could get home, change his dress, run down the bank and row down-stream to the Point, there leave his skiff and climb up to the road. He met us there at one o'clock, and the Suttons would never betray either of us, though they did not know we were engaged. We sat in their parlor a quarter of an hour after we got to town, and then 'twas time to go, and there was only a little ten minutes' walk down to the stable. I had seen him such a very short time, and I had so much to tell him." (Chester could have burst into rapturous applause had she been an actress. Her cheeks were aflame, her eyes full of fire and spirit, her bosom heaving, her little foot tapping the ground, as she stood there leaning on the colonel's fence and looking straight up in the perturbed veteran's face. She was magnificent, he said to himself; and, in her bravery, self-sacrifice, and indignation, she *was*.) "It was then after two, and I could just as well go with him,—somebody had to bring the buggy back,—and Graves himself hitched in his roan mare for me, and I drove out, picked up Mr. Jerrold at the corner, and we came out here again through the darkness together. Even when we got to the Point I did not let him go at once. It was over an hour's drive. It was fully half-past three before we parted. He sprang down the path to reach the river-side; and before he was fairly in his boat and pulling up against the stream, I heard, far over here somewhere, those two faint shots. That was the shooting he spoke of in his letter to me,—not to her; and what business Colonel Maynard had to read and exhibit to his officers a letter never intended for him I cannot understand. Mr. Jerrold says it was not what he wanted it to be at all, as he wrote hastily, so he wrote another, and sent that to me by Merrick that morning after his absence was discovered. It probably blew out of the window, as these other things did this morning. See for yourself, captain." And she pointed to the two or three bills and scraps that had evidently only recently fluttered in among the now neglected roses. "Then when he was aroused at reveille and you threatened him with punishment and held over his head the startling accusation that you knew of our meeting and our secret, he was naturally infinitely distressed, and could only write to warn me, and he managed to get in and say good-by to me at the station. As for me, I was back home by five o'clock, let myself noiselessly up to my room, and no one knew it but the Suttons and old Graves, neither of whom would betray me. I had no fear of the long dark road: I had ridden and driven as a child all over these bluffs and prairies before there was any town worth mentioning, and in days when my father and I found only friends—not enemies—here at Sibley."

"Miss Beaubien, let me protest against your accusation. It is not for me to reprove your grave imprudence or recklessness; nor have I the right to disapprove your choice of Mr. Jerrold. Let me say at once that you have none but friends here; and if it ever should be known to what lengths you went to save him, it will only make him more envied and you more genuinely admired. I question your wisdom, but, upon my soul, I admire your bravery and spirit. You have cleared him of a terrible charge."

A most disdainful and impatient shrug of her shapely shoulders was Miss Beaubien's only answer to that allusion. The possibility of Mr. Jerrold's being suspected of another entanglement was something she would not tolerate:

"I know nothing of other people's affairs. I simply speak of my own. Let us end this as quickly as possible, captain. Now about Saturday night. Mother had consented to our coming back for the german,—she enjoys seeing me lead, it seems,—and she decided to pay a short visit to relations at St. Croix, staying there Saturday night and over Sunday. This would give us a chance to meet again, as he could spend the evening in St. Croix and return by late train, and I wrote and asked him. He came; we had a long talk in the summer-house in the garden, for mother never dreamed of his being there, and unluckily he just missed the night train and did not get back until inspection. It was impossible for him to have been at Sablon; and he can furnish other proof, but would do nothing until he had seen me."

"Miss Beaubien, you have cleared him. I only wish that you could clear—every one."

"I am in no wise concerned in that other matter to which you have alluded; neither is Mr. Jerrold. May I say to him at once that this ends his persecution?"

The captain smiled: "You certainly deserve to be the bearer of good tidings. I wish he may appreciate it."

Another moment, and she had left him and sped back to Jerrold's door-way. He was there to meet her, and Chester looked with grim and uncertain emotion at the radiance in her face. He had to get back to the office and to pass them: so, as civilly as he could, considering the weight of wrath and contempt he felt for the man, he stopped and spoke:

"Your fair advocate has been all-powerful, Mr. Jerrold. I congratulate you; and your arrest is at an end. Captain Armitage will require no duty of you until we are aboard; but we've only half an hour. The train is coming sharp at noon."

"Train! What train! Where are you going?" she asked, a wild anxiety in her eyes, a sudden pallor on her face.

"We are ordered post-haste to Colorado, Nina, to rescue what is left of Thornton's men. But for you I should have been left behind."

"But for me!—left behind!" she cried. "Oh, Howard, Howard! have I only—only won you to send you into danger? Oh, my darling! Oh, God! Don't—don't go! They will kill you! It will kill me! Oh, what have I done? what have I done?"

"Nina, hush! My honor is with the regiment. I *must* go, child. We'll be back in a few weeks. Indeed, I fear 'twill all be over before we get there. *Nina*, don't look so! Don't act so! Think where you are!"

But she had borne too much, and the blow came all too soon,—too heavy. She was wellnigh senseless when the Beaubien carriage came whirling into the fort and old Maman rushed forth in voluble and rabid charge upon her daughter. All too late! it was useless now. Her darling's heart was weaned away, and her love lavished on that tall, objectionable young soldier so soon to go forth to battle. Reproaches, tears, wrath, were all in order, but were abandoned at sight of poor Nina's agony of grief. Noon came, and the train, and with buoyant tread the gallant command marched down the winding road and filed aboard the cars, and Howard Jerrold, shame-stricken, humbled at the contemplation of his own unworthiness, slowly unclasped her arms from about his neck, laid one long kiss upon her white and quivering lips, took one brief look in the great, dark, haunting, despairing eyes, and carried her wail of anguish ringing in his ears as he sprang aboard and was whirled away.

But there were women who deemed themselves worse off than Nina Beaubien,—the wives and daughters and sweethearts whom she met that morn in town; for when they got back to Sibley the regiment was miles away. For them there was not even a kiss from the lips of those they loved. Time and train waited for no woman. There were comrades battling for life in the Colorado Rockies, and aid could not come too soon.

Charles King

XVII

Under the cloudless heavens, under the starlit skies, blessing the grateful dew that cools the upland air and moistens the bunch-grass that has been bleaching all day in the fierce rays of the summer sun, a little column of infantry is swinging steadily southward. Long and toilsome has been the march; hot, dusty, and parching the day. Halts have been few and far between, and every man, from the colonel down, is coated with a gray mask of powdered alkali, the contribution of a two hours' tramp through Deadman's Canon just before the sun went down. Now, however, they are climbing the range. The morrow will bring them to the broad and beautiful valley of the Spirit Wolf, and there they must have news. Officers and men are footsore and weary, but no one begs for rest. Colonel Maynard, riding ahead on a sorry hack he picked up at the station two days' long march behind them, is eager to reach the springs at Forest Glade before ordering bivouac for the night. A week agone no one who saw him at Sablon would have thought the colonel fit for a march like this; but he seems rejuvenate. His head is high, his eye as bright, his bearing as full of spirit, as man's could possibly be at sixty, and the whole regiment cheered him when he caught the column at Omaha. A talk with Chester and Armitage seemed to have made a new man of him, and to-night he is full of an energy that inspires the entire command. Though they were farther away than many other troops ordered to the scene, the fact that their station was on the railway and that they could be sent by special trains to Omaha and thence to the West enabled them to begin their rescue-march ahead of all the other foot-troops and behind only the powerful command of cavalry that was whirled to the scene the moment the authorities woke up to the fact that it should have been sent in the first place. Old Maynard would give his very ears to get to Thornton's corral ahead of them, but the cavalry has thirty-six hours' start and four legs to two. Every moment he looks ahead expectant of tidings from the front that shall tell him the—th were there and the remnant rescued. Even then, he knows, he and his long Springfields will be needed. The cavalry can fight their way in to the succor of the besieged, but once there will be themselves surrounded and too few in numbers to begin aggressive movements. He and his will indeed be welcome reinforcements; and so they trudge ahead.

The moon is up and it is nearly ten o'clock when high up on the rolling divide the springs are reached, and, barely waiting to quench their thirst in the cooling waters, the wearied men roll themselves in their blankets under the giant trees, and, guarded by a few outlying pickets, are soon asleep. Most of the officers have sprawled around a little fire and are burning their boot-leather thereat. The colonel, his adjutant, and the doctor are curled up under a tent-fly that serves by day as a wrap for the rations and cooking-kit they carry on pack-mule. Two company commanders,—the Alpha and Omega of the ten, as Major Sloat dubbed them,—the senior and junior in rank, Chester and Armitage by name, have rolled themselves in their blankets under another tent-fly and are chatting in low tones before dropping off to sleep. They have been inseparable on the journey thus far, and the colonel has had two or three long talks with them; but who knows what the morrow may bring forth? There is still much to settle.

One officer, he of the guard, is still afoot, and trudging about among the trees, looking after his sentries. Another officer, also alone, is sitting in silence smoking a pipe: it is Mr. Jerrold.

Cleared though he is of the charges originally brought against him in the minds of his colonel and Captain Chester, he has lost caste with his fellows and with them. Only two or three men have been made aware of the statement which acquitted him, but every one knows instinctively that he was saved by Nina Beaubien, and that in accepting his release at her hands he had put her to a cruel expense. Every man among his brother officers knows in some way that he has been acquitted of having compromised Alice Renwick's fair fame only by an *alibi* that correspondingly harmed another. The fact now generally known, that they were betrothed, and that the engagement was openly announced, made no difference. Without being able to analyze his conduct, the regiment was satisfied that it had been selfish and contemptible; and that was enough to warrant giving him the cold shoulder. He was quick to see and take the hint, and, in bitter distress of mind, to withdraw himself from their companionship. He had hoped and expected that his eagerness to go with them on the wild and sudden campaign would reinstate him in their good graces, but it failed utterly. "Any man would seek *that*," was the verdict of the informal council held by the officers. "He would have been a poltroon if he hadn't sought to go; but, while he isn't a poltroon, he has done a contemptible thing." And so it stood. Rollins had cut him dead, refused his hand, and denied him a chance to explain. "Tell him he can't explain," was the savage reply he sent by the adjutant, who consented to carry Jerrold's message in order that he might have fair play. "He knows, without explanation, the wrong he has done to more than one. I won't have anything to do with him."

Others avoided him, and only coldly spoke to him when speech was necessary. Chester treated him with marked aversion; the colonel would not look at him; only Armitage—his captain—had a decent word for him at any time, and even he was stern and cold. The most envied and careless of the entire command, the Adonis, the beau, the crack shot, the graceful leader in all garrison gayeties, the beautiful dancer, rider, tennis-player, the adored of so many sentimental women at Sibley, poor Jerrold had found his level, and his proud and sensitive though selfish heart was breaking.

Sitting alone under the trees, he had taken a sheet of paper from his pocket-case and was writing by the light of the rising moon. One letter was short and easily written, for with a few words he had brought it to a close, then folded and in a bold and vigorous hand addressed it. The other was far longer; and over this one, thinking deeply, erasing some words and pondering much over others, he spent a long hour. It was nearly midnight, and he was chilled to the heart, when he stiffly rose and took his way among the blanketed groups to the camp-fire around which so many of his wearied comrades were sleeping the sleep of the tired soldier. Here he tore to fragments and scattered in the embers some notes and letters that were in his pockets. They blazed up brightly, and by the glare he stood one moment studying young Rollins's smooth and placid features; then he looked around on the unconscious circle of bronzed and bearded faces. There were many types of soldier there,—men who had led brigades through the great war and gone back to the humble bars of the line-officer at its close; men who had led fierce charges against the swarming Indians in the rough old days of the first prairie railways; men who had won distinction and honorable mention in hard and trying frontier service; men who had their faults and foibles and weaknesses like other men, and were aggressive or compliant, strong-willed or yielding, overbearing or meek, as are their brethren in other walks of life; men who were simple of heart, single in purpose and ambition, diverse in characteristics, but unanimous in one trait,—no meanness could live among them; and Jerrold's heart sank within him, colder, lower, stonier than before, as he looked from face to face and cast up mentally the sum of each man's character. His hospitality had been boundless, his bounty lavish; one and all they had eaten of his loaf and drunk of his cup; but was there among them one who could say of him, "He is generous and I stand his friend"? Was there one of them, one of theirs, for whom he had ever denied himself a pleasure, great or small? He looked at poor old Gray, with his wrinkled, anxious face, and thought of his distress of mind. Only a few thousands—not three years' pay—had the veteran scraped and saved and stored away for his little girl, whose heart was aching with its first cruel sorrow,—*his* work, *his* undoing, his cursed, selfish greed for adulation, his reckless love of love. The morrow's battle, if it came, might leave her orphaned and alone, and, poor as it was, a father's pitying sympathy could not be her help with the coming year. Would Gray mourn him if the fortune of war made *him* the victim? Would any one of those averted faces look with pity and regret upon his stiffening form? Would there be any one on earth to whom his death would be a sorrow, but Nina? Would it even be a blow to her? She loved him wildly, he knew that; but *would* she did she but dream the truth? He knew her nature well. He knew how quickly such burning love could turn to fiercest hate when convinced that the object was utterly untrue. He had said nothing to her of the photograph, nothing at all of Alice except to protest time and again that his attentions to her were solely to win the good will of the colonel's family and of the colonel himself, so that he might be proof against the machinations of his foes. And yet had he not, that very night on which he crossed the stream and let her peril her name and honor for one stolen interview—had he not gone to her exultant welcome with a traitorous knowledge gnawing at his heart? That very night, before they parted at the colonel's door had he not lied to Alice Renwick?—had he not denied the story of his devotion to Miss Beaubien, and was not his practised eye watching eagerly the beautiful dark face for one sign that the news was welcome, and so precipitate the avowal trembling on his lips that it was *her* he madly loved,—not Nina? Though she hurriedly bade him good-night, though she was unprepared for any such announcement, he well knew that Alice Renwick's heart fluttered at the earnestness of his manner, and that he had indicated far more than he had said. Fear—not love—had drawn him to Nina Beaubien that night, and hope had centred on her more beautiful rival, when the discoveries of the night involved him in the first trembling symptoms of the downfall to come. And he was to have spent the morning with her, the woman to whom he had lied in word, while she to whom he had lied in word and deed was going from him, not to return until the german, and even then he planned treachery. He meant to lead with Alice Renwick and claim that it *must* be with the colonel's daughter because the ladies of the garrison were the givers. Then, he knew, Nina would not come at all, and, possibly, might quarrel with him on that ground. What could have been an easier solution of his troublous predicament? She would break their secret engagement; he would refuse all reconciliation, and be free to devote himself to Alice. But all these grave complications had arisen. Alice would not come. Nina wrote demanding that he should lead with her, and that he should meet her at St. Croix; and then came the crash. He owed his safety to her self-sacrifice, and now must give up all hope of Alice Renwick. He had accepted the announcement of their engagement. He *could* not do less, after all that had happened and the painful scene at their parting. And yet would it not be a blessing to her if he were killed? Even now in his self-abnegation and misery he did not fully realize how mean he was,—how mean he seemed to others. He resented in his heart what Sloat had said of him but the day before, little caring whether he heard it or not: "It would be a mercy to that poor girl if Jerrold were killed. He will break her heart with neglect, or drive her mad with jealousy, inside of a year." But the regiment seemed to agree with Sloat.

And so in all that little band of comrades he could call no man friend. One after another he looked upon the unconscious faces, cold and averted in the oblivion of sleep, but not more cold, not more distrustful, than when he had vainly sought among them one relenting glance in the early moonlight that battle eve in bivouac. He threw his arms upward, shook his head with hopeless gesture, then buried his face in the sleeves of his rough campaign overcoat and strode blindly from their midst.

Early in the morning, an hour before daybreak, the shivering out-post crouching in a hollow to the southward catch sight of two dim figures shooting suddenly up over a distant ridge,—horsemen, they know at a glance,—and these two come loping down the moonlit trail over which two nights before had marched the cavalry speeding to the rescue, over which in an hour the regiment itself must be on the move. Old campaigners are two of the picket, and they have been especially cautioned to be on the lookout for couriers coming back along the trail. They spring to their feet, in readiness to welcome or repel, as the sentry rings out his sharp and sudden challenge.

"Couriers from the corral," is the jubilant answer. "This Colonel Maynard's outfit?"

"Ay, ay, sonny," is the unmilitary but characteristic answer. "What's your news?"

"Got there in time, and saved what's left of 'em; but it's a hell-hole, and you fellows are wanted quick as you can come,—thirty miles ahead. Where's the colonel?"

The corporal of the guard goes back to the bivouac, leading the two arrivals. One is a scout, a plainsman born and bred, the other a sergeant of cavalry. They dismount in the timber and picket their horses, then follow on foot the lead of their companion of the guard. While the corporal and the scout proceed to the wagon-fly and fumble at the opening, the tall sergeant stands silently a little distance in their rear, and the occupants of a neighboring shelter—the counterpart of the colonel's—begin to stir, as though their light slumber had been broken by the smothered sound of footsteps. One of them sits up and peers out at the front, gazing earnestly at the tall figure standing easily there in the flickering light. Then he hails in low tones:

"That you, Mr. Jerrold? What is the matter?"

And the tall figure faces promptly towards the hailing voice. The spurred heels come together with a click, the gauntleted hand rises in soldierly salute to the broad brim of the scouting-hat, and a deep voice answers, respectfully,—

"It is not Mr. Jerrold, sir. It is Sergeant McLeod,—th Cavalry, just in with despatches."

Armitage springs to his feet, sheds his shell of blankets, and steps forth into the glade with his eyes fixed eagerly on the shadowy form in front. He peers under the broad brim, as though striving to see the eyes and features of the tall dragoon.

"Did you get there in time?" he asks, half wondering whether that was really the question uppermost in his mind.

"In time to save the survivors, sir; but no attack will be made until the infantry get there."

"Were you not at Sibley last month?" asks the captain, quickly.

"Yes, sir,—with the competitors."

"You went back before your regimental team, did you not?"

"I—No, sir: I went back with them."

"You were relieved from duty at Sibley and ordered back before them, were you not?"

Even in the pallid light Armitage could see the hesitation, the flurry of surprise and distress, in the sergeant's face.

"Don't fear to tell me, man: I would rather hear it than any news you could give me. I would rather know you were *not* Sergeant McLeod than any fact you could tell. Speak low, man, but tell me here and now. Whatever motive you may have had for this disguise, whatever anger or sorrows in the past, you must sink them now to save the honor of the woman your madness has perilled. Answer me, for your sister's sake: are you not Fred Renwick?"

"Do you swear to me she is in danger?"

"By all that's sacred; and you ought to know it."

"I *am* Fred Renwick. Now what can I do?"

XVIII

The sun is not an hour high, but the bivouac at the springs is far behind. With advance-guard and flankers well out, the regiment is tramping its way, full of eagerness and spirit. The men can hardly refrain from bursting into song, but, although at "route step," the fact that Indian scouts have already been sighted scurrying from bluff to bluff is sufficient to warn all hands to be silent and alert. Wilton with his company is on the dangerous flank, and guards it well. Armitage with Company B covers the advance, and his men are strung out in long skirmish-line across the trail wherever the ground is sufficiently open to admit of deployment. Where it is not, they spring ahead and explore every point where Indian may lurk, and render ambuscade of the main column impossible. With Armitage is McLeod, the cavalry sergeant who made the night ride with the scout who bore the despatches. The scout has galloped on towards the railway with news of the rescue, the sergeant guides the infantry reinforcement. Observant men have noted that Armitage and the sergeant have had a vast deal to say to each other during the chill hours of the early morn. Others have noted that at the first brief halt the captain rode back, called Colonel Maynard to one side, and spoke to him in low tones. The colonel was seen to start with astonishment. Then he said a few words to his second in command, and rode forward with Armitage to join the advance. When the regiment moved on again and the head of column hove in sight of the skirmishers, they saw that the colonel, Armitage, and the sergeant of cavalry were riding side by side, and that the officers were paying close attention to all the dragoon was saying. All were eager to hear the particulars of the condition of affairs at the corral, and all were disposed to be envious of the mounted captain who could ride alongside the one participant in the rescuing charge and get it all at first hand. The field-officers, of course, were mounted, but every line-officer marched afoot with his men, except that three horses had been picked up at the railway and impressed by the quartermaster in case of need, and these were assigned to the captains who happened to command the skirmishers and flankers.

But no man had the faintest idea what manner of story that tall sergeant was telling. It would have been of interest to every soldier in the command, but to no one so much so as to the two who were his absorbed listeners. Armitage, before their early march, had frankly and briefly set before him his suspicions as to the case, and the trouble in which Miss Renwick was involved. No time was to be lost. Any moment might find them plunged in fierce battle; and who could foretell the results?—who could say what might happen to prevent this her vindication ever reaching the ears of her accusers? Some men wondered why it was that Colonel Maynard sent his compliments to Captain Chester and begged that at the next halt he would join him. The halt did not come for a long hour, and when it did come it was very brief, but Chester received another message, and went forward to find his colonel sitting in a little grove with the cavalryman, while the orderly held their horses a short space away. Armitage had gone forward to his advance, and Chester showed no surprise at the sight of the sergeant seated side by side with the colonel and in confidential converse with him. There was a quaint, sly twinkle in Maynard's eyes as he greeted his old friend.

"Chester," said he, "I want you to be better acquainted with my step-son, Mr. Renwick. He has an apology to make to you."

The tall soldier had risen the instant he caught sight of the newcomer, and even at the half-playful tone of the colonel would relax in no degree his soldierly sense of the proprieties. He stood erect and held his hand at the salute, only very slowly lowering it to take the one so frankly extended him by the captain, who, however, was grave and quiet.

"I have suspected as much since daybreak," he said; "and no man is gladder to know it is you than I am."

"You would have known it before, sir, had I had the faintest idea of the danger in which my foolhardiness had involved my sister. The colonel has told you of my story. I have told him and Captain Armitage what led to my mad freak at Sibley; and, while I have much to make amends for, I want to apologize for the blow I gave you that night on the terrace. I was far more scared than you were, sir."

"I think we can afford to forgive him, Chester. He knocked us both out," said the colonel.

Chester bowed gravely. "That was the easiest part of the affair to forgive," he said, "and it is hardly for me, I presume, to be the only one to blame the sergeant for the trouble that has involved us all, especially your household, colonel."

"It was expensive masquerading, to say the least," replied the colonel; "but he never realized the consequences until Armitage told him to-day. You must hear his story in brief, Chester. It is needful that three or four of us know it, so that some may be left to set things right at Sibley. God grant us all safe return!" he added, piously, and with deep emotion. "I can far better appreciate our home and happiness than I could a month ago. Now, Renwick, tell the captain what you have told us."

And briefly it *was* told: how in his youthful fury he had sworn never again to set foot within the door of the father and mother who had so wronged the poor girl he loved with boyish fervor; how he called down the vengeance of heaven upon them in his frenzy and distress; how he had sworn never again to set eyes on their faces. "May God strike me dead if ever I return to this roof until she is avenged! May He deal with you as you have dealt with her!" was the curse that flew from his wild lips, and with that he left them, stunned. He went West, was soon penniless, and, caring not what he did, seeking change, adventure, anything to take him out of his past, he enlisted in the cavalry, and was speedily drafted to the—th, which was just starting forth on a stirring summer campaign. He was a fine horseman, a fine shot, a man who instantly attracted the notice of his officers: the campaign was full of danger, adventure, rapid and constant marching, and before he knew it or dreamed it possible he had become deeply interested in his new life. Only in the monotony of a month or two in garrison that winter did the service seem intolerable. His comrades were rough, in the main, but thoroughly good-hearted, and he soon won their esteem. The spring sent them again into the field; another stirring campaign, and here he won his stripes, and words of praise from the lips of a veteran general officer, as well as the promise of future reward; and then the love of soldierly deeds and the thirst for soldierly renown took firm hold in his breast. He began to turn towards the mother and father who had been wrapped up in his future,—who loved him so devotedly. He was forgetting his early and passionate love, and the bitter sorrow of her death was losing fast its poignant power to steel him against his kindred. He knew they could not but be proud of the record he had made in the ranks of the gallant—th, and then he shrank and shivered when he recalled the dreadful words of his curse. He had made up his mind to write, implore pardon for his hideous and unfilial language, and invoke their interest in his career, when, returning to Fort Raines for supplies, he picked up a New York paper in the reading-room and read the announcement of his father's death, "whose health had been broken ever since the disappearance of his only son, two years before." The memory of his malediction had, indeed, come home to him, and he fell, stricken by a sudden and unaccountable blow. It seemed as though his heart had given one wild leap, then stopped forever. Things did not go so well after this. He brooded over his words, and believed that an avenging God had launched the bolt that killed the father as punishment to the stubborn and recreant son. He then bethought him of his mother, of pretty Alice, who had loved him so as a little girl. He could not bring himself to write, but through inquiries he learned that the house was closed and that they had gone abroad. He plodded on in his duties a trying year: then came more lively field-work and reviving interest. He was forgetting entirely the sting of his first great sorrow, and mourning gravely the gulf he had placed 'twixt him and his. He thought time and again of his cruel words, and something began to whisper to him he must see that mother again at once, kiss her hand, and implore her forgiveness, or she, too, would be stricken suddenly. He saved up his money, hoping that after the summer's rifle-work at Sibley he might get a furlough and go East; and the night he arrived at the fort, tired with his long railway-journey and panting after a long and difficult climb up-hill, his mother's face swam suddenly before his eyes, and he felt himself going down. When they brought him to, he heard that the ladies were Mrs. Maynard and her daughter Miss Renwick,—his own mother, remarried, his own Alice, a grown young woman. This was, indeed, news to put him in a flutter and spoil his shooting. He realized at once that the gulf was wider than ever. How could he go to her now, the wife of a colonel, and he an enlisted man? Like other soldiers, he forgot that the line of demarcation was one of discipline, not of sympathy. He did not realize what any soldier among his officers would gladly have told him, that he was most worthy to reveal himself now,—a non-commissioned officer whose record was an honor to himself and to his regiment, a soldier of whom officers and comrades alike were proud. He never dreamed—indeed, how few there are who do!—that a man of his character, standing, and ability is honored and respected by the very men whom the customs of the service require him to speak with only when spoken to. He supposed that only as Fred Renwick could he extend his hand to one of their number, whereas it was under his soldier name he won their trust and admiration, and it was as Sergeant McLeod the officers of the—th were backing him for a commission that would make him what they deemed him fit to be,—their equal. Unable to penetrate the armor of reserve and discipline which separates the officer from the rank and file, he never imagined that the colonel would have been the first to welcome him had he known the truth. He believed that now his last chance of seeing his mother was gone until that coveted commission was won. Then came another blow: the doctor told him that with his heart-trouble he could never pass the physical examination: he could not hope for preferment, then, and *must* see her as he was, and see her secretly and alone. Then came blow after blow. His shooting had failed, so had that of others of his regiment, and he was ordered to return in charge of the party early on the morrow. The order reached him late in the evening, and before breakfast-time on the following day he was directed to start with his party for town, thence by rail to his distant post. That night, in desperation, he made his plan. Twice before he had strolled down to the post and with yearning eyes had studied every feature of the colonel's house. He dared ask no questions of servants or of the men in garrison, but he learned enough to know which rooms were theirs, and he had noted that the windows were always open. If he could only see their loved faces, kneel and kiss his mother's hand, pray God to forgive him, he could go away believing that he had undone the spell and revoked the malediction of his early youth. It was hazardous, but worth the danger. He could go in peace and sin no more towards mother, at least; and then if she mourned and missed him, could he not find it out some day and make himself known to her after his discharge? He slipped out of camp, leaving his boots behind, and wearing his light Apache moccasins and flannel shirt and trousers. Danger to himself he had no great fear of. If by any chance mother or sister should wake, he had but to stretch forth his hand and say, "It is only I,—Fred." Danger to *them* he never dreamed of.

Strong and athletic, despite his slender frame, he easily lifted the ladder from Jerrold's fence, and, dodging the sentry when he spied him at the gate, finally took it down back of the colonel's and raised it to a rear window. By the strangest chance the window was closed, and he could not budge it. Then he heard the challenge of a sentry around on the east front, and had just time to slip down and lower the ladder when he heard the rattle of a sword and knew it must be the officer of the day. There was no time to carry off the ladder. He left it lying where it was, and sprang down the steps towards the station. Soon he heard Number Five challenge, and knew the officer had passed on: he waited some time, but nothing occurred to indicate that the ladder was discovered, and then, plucking up courage and with a muttered prayer for guidance and protection, he stole up-hill again, raised the ladder to the west wall, noiselessly ascended, peered in Alice's window and could see a faint night-light burning in the hall beyond, but that all was darkness there, stole around on the roof of the piazza to the hall window, stepped noiselessly upon the sill, climbed over the lowered sash, and found himself midway between the rooms. He could hear the colonel's placid snoring and the regular breathing of the other sleepers. No time was to be lost. Shading the little night-lamp with one hand, he entered the open door, stole to the bedside, took one long look at his mother's face, knelt, breathed upon, but barely brushed with his trembling lips, the queenly white hand that lay upon the coverlet, poured forth one brief prayer to God for protection and blessing for her and forgiveness for him, retraced his steps, and caught sight of the lovely picture of Alice in the Directoire costume. He longed for it and could not resist. She had grown so beautiful, so exquisite. He took it, frame and all, carried it into her room, slipped the card from its place and hid it inside the breast of his shirt, stowed the frame away behind her sofa-pillow, then looked long at the lovely picture she herself made, lying there sleeping sweetly and peacefully amid the white drapings of her dainty bed. Then 'twas time to go. He put the lamp back in the hall, passed through her room, out at her window, and down the ladder, and had it well on the way back to the hooks on Jerrold's fence when seized and challenged by the officer of the day. Mad terror possessed him then. He struck blindly, dashed off in panicky flight, paid no heed to sentry's cry or whistling missile, but tore like a racer up the path and never slackened speed till Sibley was far behind.

When morning came, the order that they should go was temporarily suspended: some prisoners were sent to a neighboring military prison, and he was placed in charge, and on his return from this duty learned that the colonel's family had gone to Sablon. The next thing there was some strange talk that worried him,—a story that one of the men who had a sweetheart who was second girl at Mrs. Hoyt's brought out to camp,—a story that there was an officer who was too much in love with Alice to keep away from the house even after the colonel so ordered, and that he was prowling around the other night and the colonel ordered Leary to shoot him,—Leary, who was on post on Number Five. He felt sure that something was wrong,—felt sure that it was due to his night visit,—and his first impulse was to find his mother and confide the truth to her. He longed to see her again, and if harm had been done, to make himself known and explain everything. Having no duties to detain him, he got a pass to visit town and permission to be gone a day or more. On Saturday evening he ran down to Sablon, drove over, as Captain Armitage had already told them, and, peering in his mother's room, saw her, still up, though in her nightdress. He never dreamed of the colonel's being out and watching. He had "scouted" all those trees, and no one was nigh. Then he softly called; she heard, and was coming to him, when again came fierce attack: he had all a soldier's reverence for the person of the colonel, and would never have harmed him had he known 'twas he: it was the night watchman that had grappled with him, he supposed, and he had no compunctions in sending him to grass. Then he fled again, knowing that he had only made bad worse, walked all that night to the station next north of Sablon,—a big town where the early morning train always stopped,—and by ten on Sunday morning he was in uniform again and off with his regimental comrades under orders to haste to their station,— there was trouble with the Indians at Spirit Rock and the—th were held in readiness. From beneath his scouting-shirt he drew a flat packet, an Indian case, which he carefully unrolled, and there in its folds of wrappings was the lovely Directoire photograph.

Whose, then, was the one that Sloat had seen in Jerrold's room? It was this that Armitage had gone forward to determine, and he found his sad-eyed lieutenant with the skirmishers.

"Jerrold," said he, with softened manner, "a strange thing is brought to light this morning, and I lose no time in telling you. The man who was seen at Maynard's quarters, coming from Miss Renwick's room, was her own brother and the colonel's step-son. He was the man who took the photograph from Mrs. Maynard's room, and has proved it this very day,—this very hour." Jerrold glanced up in sudden surprise. "He is with us now, and only one thing remains, which you can clear up. We are going into action, and I may not get through, nor you, nor—who knows who? Will you tell us now how you came by your copy of that photograph?"

For answer Jerrold fumbled in his pocket a moment and drew forth two letters:

"I wrote these last night, and it was my intention to see that you had them before it grew very hot. One is addressed to you, the other to Miss Beaubien. You had better take them now," he said, wearily. "There may be no time to talk after this. Send hers after it's over, and don't read yours until then."

"Why, I don't understand this, exactly," said Armitage, puzzled. "Can't you tell me about the picture?"

"No. I promised not to while I lived; but it's the simplest matter in the world, and no one at the colonel's had any hand in it. They never saw this one that I got to show Sloat. It is burned now. I said 'twas given me. That was hardly the truth. I have paid for it dearly enough."

"And this note explains it?"

"Yes. You can read it to-morrow."

XIX

And the morrow has come. Down in a deep and bluff-shadowed valley, hung all around with picturesque crags and pine-crested heights, under a cloudless September sun whose warmth is tempered by the mountain-breeze, a thousand rough-looking, bronzed and bearded and powder-blackened men are resting after battle.

Here and there on distant ridge and point the cavalry vedettes keep vigilant watch, against surprise or renewed attack. Down along the banks of a clear, purling stream a sentry paces slowly by the brown line of rifles, swivel-stacked in the sunshine. Men by the dozen are washing their blistered feet and grimy hands and faces in the cool, refreshing water; men by the dozen lie soundly sleeping, some in the broad glare, some in the shade of the little clump of willows, all heedless of the pestering swarms of flies. Out on the broad, grassy slopes, side-lined and watched by keen-eyed guards, the herds of cavalry horses are quietly grazing, forgetful of the wild excitement of yester-even. Every now and then some one of them lifts his head, pricks up his ears, and snorts and stamps suspiciously as he sniffs at the puffs of smoke that come drifting up the valley from the fires a mile away. The waking men, too, bestow an occasional comment on the odor which greets their nostrils. Down-stream where the fires are burning are the blackened remnants of a wagon-train:

tires, bolts, and axles are lying about, but all wood-work is in smouldering ashes; so, too, is all that remains of several hundred-weight of stores and supplies destined originally to nourish the Indians, but, by them, diverted to feed the fire.

There is a big circle of seething flame and rolling smoke here, too,—a malodorous neighborhood, around which fatigue-parties are working with averted heads; and among them some surly and unwilling Indians, driven to labor at the muzzle of threatening revolver or carbine, aid in dragging to the flames carcass after carcass of horse and mule, and in gathering together and throwing on the pyre an array of miscellaneous soldier garments, blouses, shirts, and trousers, all more or less hacked and blood-stained,—all of no more use to mortal wearer.

Out on the southern slopes, just where a ravine crowded with wild-rose bushes opens into the valley, more than half the command is gathered, formed in rectangular lines about a number of shallow, elongated pits, in each of which there lies the stiffening form of a comrade who but yesterday joined in the battle-cheer that burst upon the valley with the setting sun. Silent and reverent they stand in their rough campaign garb. The escort of infantry "rests on arms;" the others bow their uncovered heads, and it is the voice of the veteran colonel that, in accents trembling with sympathy and emotion, renders the last tribute to fallen comrades and lifts to heaven the prayers for the dead. Then see! The mourning groups break away from the southern side; the brown rifles of the escort are lifted in air; the listening rocks resound to the sudden ring of the flashing volley; the soft, low, wailing good-by of the trumpets goes floating up the vale, and soon the burial-parties are left alone to cover the once familiar faces with the earth to which the soldier must return, and the comrades who are left, foot and dragoon, come marching, silent, back to camp.

And when the old regiment begins its homeward journey, leaving the well-won field to the fast-arriving commands and bidding hearty soldier farewell to the cavalry comrades whose friendship they gained in the front of a savage foe, the company that was the first to land its fire in the fight goes back with diminished numbers and under command of its second lieutenant. Alas, poor Jerrold!

There is a solemn little group around the camp-fire the night before they go. Frank Armitage, flat on his back, with a rifle-bullet through his thigh, but taking things very coolly for all that, is having a quiet conference with his colonel. Such of the wounded of the entire command as are well enough to travel by easy stages to the railway go with Maynard and the regiment in the morning, and Sergeant McLeod, with his sabre-arm in a sling, is one of these. But the captain of Company B must wait until the surgeons can lift him along in an ambulance and all fear of fever has subsided. To the colonel and Chester he hands the note which is all that is left to comfort poor Nina Beaubien. To them he reads aloud the note addressed to himself:

"You are right in saying that the matter of my possession of that photograph should be explained. I seek no longer to palliate my action. In making that puppyish bet with Sloat I *did* believe that I could induce Miss Renwick or her mother to let me have a copy; but I was refused so positively that I knew it was useless. This simply added to my desire to have one. The photographer was the same that took the pictures and furnished the albums for our class at graduation, and I, more than any one, had been instrumental in getting the order for him against very active opposition. He had always professed the greatest gratitude to me and a willingness to do anything for me. I wrote to him in strict confidence, told him of the intimate and close relations existing between the colonel's family and me, told him I wanted it to enlarge and present to her mother on her approaching birthday, and promised him that I would never reveal how I came by the picture so long as I lived; and he sent me one,—just in time. Have I not paid heavily for my sin?"

No one spoke for a moment. Chester was the first to break the silence:

"Poor fellow! He kept his word to the photographer; but what was it worth to a woman?"

There had been a week of wild anxiety and excitement at Sibley. It was known through the columns of the press that the regiment had hurried forward from the railway the instant it reached the Colorado trail, that it could not hope to get through to the valley of the Spirit Wolf without a fight, and that the moment it succeeded in joining hands with the cavalry already there a vigorous attack would be made on the Indians. The news of the rescue of the survivors of Thornton's command came first, and with it the tidings that Maynard and his regiment were met only thirty miles from the scene and were pushing forward. The next news came two days later, and a wail went up even while men were shaking hands and rejoicing over the gallant fight that had been made, and women were weeping for joy and thanking God that those whom they held dearest were safe. It was down among the wives of the sergeants and other veterans that the blow struck hardest at Sibley; for the stricken officers were unmarried men, while among the rank and file there were several who never came back to the little ones who bore their name. Company B had suffered most, for the Indians had charged fiercely on its deployed but steadfast line. Armitage almost choked and broke down when telling the colonel about it that night as he lay under the willows: "It was the first smile I had seen on his face since I got back,— that with which he looked up in my eyes and whispered good-by,—and died,—just after we drove them back. My turn came later." Old Sloat, too, "had his customary crack," as he expressed it,—a shot through the wrist that made him hop and swear savagely until some of the men got to laughing at the comical figure he cut, and then he turned and damned them with hearty good will, and seemed all oblivious of the bullets that went zipping past his frosting head. Young Rollins, to his inexpressible pride and comfort, had a bullet-hole through his scouting-hat and another through his shoulder-strap that raised a big welt on the white skin beneath, but, to the detriment of promotion, no captain was killed, and Jerrold gave the only file.

The one question at Sibley was, "What will Nina Beaubien do?"

She did nothing. She would see nobody from the instant the news came. She had hardly slept at night,—was always awake at dawn and out at the gate to get the earliest copy of the morning papers; but the news reached them at nightfall, and when some of the ladies from the fort drove in to offer their sympathy and condolence in the morning, and to make tender inquiry, the answer at the door was that Miss Nina saw nobody, that her mother alone was with her, and that "she was very still." And so it went for some days. Then there came the return of the command to Sibley; and hundreds of people went up from town to see the six companies of the fort garrison march up the winding road amid the thunder of welcome from the guns of the light battery and the exultant strains of the band. Mrs. Maynard and Alice were the only ladies of the circle who were not there: a son and brother had joined them, after long absence, at Aunt Grace's cottage at Sablon, was the explanation, and the colonel would bring them home in a few days, after he had attended to some important matters at the fort. In the first place, Chester had to see to it that the tongue of scandal was slit, so far as the colonel's household was concerned, and all good people notified that no such thing had happened as was popularly supposed (and "everybody" received the announcement with the remark that she knew all along it couldn't be so), and that a grievous and absurd but most mortifying blunder had been made. It was a most unpleasant ghost to "down," the shadow of that scandal, for it would come up to the surface of garrison chat at all manner of confidential moments; but no man or woman could safely speak of it to Chester. It was gradually assumed that he was the man who had done all the blundering and that he was supersensitive on the subject.

There was another thing never satisfactorily explained to some of the garrison people, and that was Nina Beaubien's strange conduct. In less than a week she was seen on the street in colors,—brilliant colors,—when it was known she had ordered deep mourning, and then she suddenly disappeared and went with her silent old mother abroad. To this day no woman in society understands it, for when she came back, long, long afterwards, it was a subject on which she would never speak. There were one or two who ventured to ask, and the answer was, "For reasons that concern me alone." But it took no great power of mental vision to see that her heart wore black for him forever.

His letter explained it all. She had received it with a paroxysm of passionate grief and joy, kissed it, covered it with wildest caresses before she began to read, and then, little by little, as the words unfolded before her staring eyes, turned cold as stone:

"It is my last night of life, Nina, and I am glad 'tis so. Proud and sensitive as I am, the knowledge that every man in my regiment has turned from me,—that I have not a friend among them,—that there is no longer a place for me in their midst,—more than all, that I *deserve* their contempt,—has broken my heart. We will be in battle before the setting of another sun. Any man who seeks death in Indian fight can find it easily enough, and I can *compel* their respect in spite of themselves. They will not recognize me, living, as one of them; but dying on the field, they have to place me on their roll of honor.

"But now I turn to you. What have I been,—what am I,—to have won such love as yours? May God in heaven forgive me for my past! All too late I hate and despise the man I have been,—the man whom you loved. One last act of justice remains. If I died without it you would mourn me faithfully, tenderly, lovingly, for years, but if I tell the truth you will see the utter unworthiness of the man, and your love will turn to contempt. It is hard to do this, knowing that in doing it I kill the only genuine regret and dry the only tear that would bless my memory; but it is the one sacrifice I can make to complete my self-humiliation, and it is the one thing that is left me that will free you. It will sting at first, but, like the surgeon's knife, its cut is mercy. Nina, the very night I came to you on the bluffs, the very night you perilled your honor to have that parting interview, I went to you with a lie on my lips. I had told *her* we were nothing to each other,— you and I. More than that, I was seeking her love; I hoped I could win her; and had she loved me I would have turned from you to make her my wife. Nina, I loved Alice Renwick. Good-by. Don't mourn for me after this."

XX

They were having a family conclave at Sablon. The furlough granted Sergeant McLeod on account of wound received in action with hostile Indians would soon expire, and the question was, should he ask an extension, apply for a discharge, or go back and rejoin his troop? It was a matter on which there was much diversity of opinion. Mrs. Maynard should naturally be permitted first choice, and to her wish there was every reason for according deep and tender consideration. No words can tell of the rapture of that reunion with her long-lost son. It was a scene over which the colonel could never ponder without deep emotion. The telegrams and letters by which he carefully prepared her for Frederick's coming were all insufficient. She knew well that her boy must have greatly changed and matured, but when this tall, bronzed, bearded, stalwart man sprang from the old red omnibus and threw his one serviceable arm around her trembling form, the mother was utterly overcome. Alice left them alone together a full hour before even she intruded, and little by little, as the days went by and Mrs. Maynard realized that it was really her Fred who was whistling about, the cottage or booming trooper songs in his great basso profundo, and glorying in his regiment and the cavalry life he had led, a wonderful content and joy shone in her handsome face. It was not until the colonel announced that it was about time for them to think of going back to Sibley that the cloud came. Fred said *he* couldn't go.

In fact, the colonel himself had been worrying a little over it. As Fred Renwick, the tall distinguished young man in civilian costume, he would be welcome anywhere; but, though his garb was that of the sovereign citizen so long as his furlough lasted, there were but two weeks more of it left, and officially he was nothing more nor less than Sergeant McLeod, Troop B,—th Cavalry, and there was no precedent for a colonel's entertaining as an honored guest and social equal one of the enlisted men of the army. He rather hoped that Fred would yield to his mother's entreaties and apply for a discharge. His wound and the latent trouble with his heart would probably render it an easy matter to obtain; and yet he was ashamed of himself for the feeling.

Then there was Alice. It was hardly to be supposed that so very high bred a young woman would relish the idea of being seen around Fort Sibley on the arm of her brother the sergeant; but, wonderful to relate, Miss Alice took a radically different view of the whole situation. So far from wishing Fred out of the army, she importuned him day after day until he got out his best uniform, with its resplendent chevrons and stripes of vivid yellow, and the yellow helmet-cords, though they were but humble worsted, and when he came forth in that dress, with the bronze medal on his left breast and the sharpshooter's silver cross, his tall athletic figure showing to such advantage, his dark, Southern, manly features so enhanced by contrast with his yellow facings, she clapped her hands with a cry of delight and sprang into his one available arm and threw her own about his neck and kissed him again and again. Even mamma had to admit he looked astonishingly well; but Alice declared she would never thereafter be reconciled to seeing him in anything but a cavalry uniform. The colonel found her not at all of her mother's way of thinking. She saw no reason why Fred should leave the service. Other sergeants had won their commissions every year: why not he? Even if it were some time in coming, was there shame or degradation in being a cavalry sergeant? Not a bit of it! Fred himself was loath to quit. He was getting a little homesick, too,—homesick for the boundless life and space and air of the broad frontier,— homesick for the rapid movement and vigorous hours in the saddle and on the scout. His arm was healing, and such a delight of a letter had come from his captain, telling him that the adjutant had just been to see him about the new staff of the regiment. The gallant sergeant-major, a young Prussian of marked ability, had been killed early in the campaign; the vacancy must soon be filled, and the colonel and the adjutant both thought at once of Sergeant McLeod. "I won't stand in your way, sergeant," wrote his troop commander, "but you know that old Ryan is to be discharged at the end of his sixth enlistment the 10th of next month; there is no man I would sooner see in his place as first sergeant of my troop than yourself, and I hate to lose you; but, as it will be for the gain and the good of the whole regiment, you ought to accept the adjutant's offer. All the men rejoice to hear you are recovering so fast, and all will be glad to see Sergeant McLeod back again."

Even Mrs. Maynard could not but see the pride and comfort this letter gave her son. Her own longing was to have him established in some business in the East; but he said frankly he had no taste for it, and would only pine for the old life in the saddle. There were other reasons, too, said he, why he felt that he could not go back to New York, and his voice trembled, and Mrs. Maynard said no more. It was the sole allusion he had made to the old, old sorrow, but it was plain that the recovery was incomplete. The colonel and the doctor at Sibley believed that Fred could be carried past the medical board by a little management, and everything began to look as though he would have his way. All they were waiting for, said the colonel, was to hear from Armitage. He was still at Fort Russell with the head-quarters and several troops of the—th Cavalry: his wound was too severe for him to travel farther for weeks to come, but he could write, and he had been consulted. They were sitting under the broad piazza at Sablon, looking out at the lovely, placid lake, and talking it over among themselves.

"I have always leaned on Armitage ever since I first came to the regiment and found him adjutant," said the colonel. "I always found his judgment clear; but since our last experience I have begun to look upon him as infallible."

Alice Renwick's face took on a flood of crimson as she sat there by her brother's side, silent and attentive. Only within the week that followed their return—the colonel's and her brother's—had the story of the strange complication been revealed to them. Twice had she heard from Fred's lips the story of Frank Armitage's greeting that frosty morning at the springs. Time and again had she made her mother go over the colonel's account of the confidence and faith he had expressed in there being a simple explanation of the whole mystery, and of his indignant refusal to attach one moment's suspicion to her. Shocked, stunned, outraged as she felt at the mere fact that such a story had gained an instant's credence in garrison circles, she was overwhelmed by the weight of circumstantial evidence that had been arrayed against her. Only little by little did her mother reveal it to her. Only after several days did Fred repeat the story of his night adventure and his theft of her picture, of his narrow escape, and of his subsequent visit to the cottage. Only gradually had her mother revealed to her the circumstances of Jerrold's wager with Sloat, and the direful consequences; of his double absences the very nights on which Fred had made his visits; of the suspicions that resulted, the accusations, and his refusal to explain and clear her name. Mrs. Maynard felt vaguely relieved to see how slight an impression the young man had made on her daughter's heart. Alice seemed but little surprised to hear of the engagement to Nina Beaubien, of her rush to his rescue, and their romantic parting. The tragedy of his death hushed all further talk on that subject. There was one on which she could not hear enough, and that was about the man who had been most instrumental in the rescue of her name and honor. Alice had only tender sorrow and no reproach for her step-father when, after her mother told her the story of his sad experience twenty years before, she related his distress of mind and suspicion when he read Jerrold's letter. It was then that Alice said, "And against that piece of evidence no man, I suppose, would hold me guiltless."

"You are wrong, dear," was her mother's answer. "It was powerless to move Captain Armitage. He scouted the idea of your guilt from the moment he set eyes on you, and never rested until he had overturned the last atom of evidence. Even I had to explain," said her mother "simply to confirm his theory of the light Captain Chester had seen and the shadows and the form at the window. It was just exactly as Armitage reasoned it out. I was wretched and wakeful, sleeping but fitfully, that night. I arose and took some bromide about three o'clock and soon afterwards heard a fall, or a noise like one. I thought of you and got up and went in your room, and all was quiet there, but it seemed close and warm: so I raised your shade, and then left both your door and mine open and went back to bed. I dozed away presently, and then woke feeling all startled again,—don't you know?—the sensation one experiences when aroused from sleep, certain that there has been a strange and startling noise, and yet unable to tell what it was? I lay still a moment, but the colonel slept through it all, and I wondered at it. I knew there had been a shot, or something, but could not bear to disturb him. At last I got up again and went to your room to be sure you were all right, and you were sleeping soundly still; but a breeze was beginning to blow and flap your shade to and fro, so I drew it and went out, taking my lamp with me this time and softly closing your door behind me. See how it all seemed to fit in with everything else that had happened. It took a man with a will of his own and an unshaken faith in woman to stand firm against such evidence."

And, though Alice Renwick was silent, she appreciated the fact none the less. Day after day she clung to her stalwart brother's side. She had ceased to ask questions about Captain Armitage and the strange greeting after the first day or two, but, oddly enough, she could never let him talk long of any subject but that campaign, of his ride with the captain to the front, of the long talk they had had, and the stirring fight and the magnificent way in which Armitage had handled his long skirmish-line. He was enthusiastic in his praise of the tall Saxon captain. He soon noted how silent and absorbed she sat when he was the theme of discourse; he incidentally mentioned little things "he" had said about "her" that morning, and marked how her color rose and her eyes flashed quick, joyful, questioning glance at his face, then fell in maiden shyness. He had speedily gauged the cause of that strange excitement displayed by Armitage at seeing him the morning he rode in with the scout. Now he was gauging, with infinite delight, the other side of the question. The brother-like, he began to twit and tease her; and that was the last of the confidences.

All the same it was an eager group that surrounded the colonel the evening he came down with the captain's letter. "It settles the thing in my mind. We'll go back to Sibley to-morrow; and as for you, Sergeant-Major Fred, your name has gone in for a commission, and I've no doubt a very deserving sergeant will be spoiled in making a very good-for-nothing second lieutenant. Get you back to your regiment, sir, and call on Captain Armitage as soon as you reach Fort Russell, and tell him you are much obliged. He has been blowing your trumpet for you there; and, as some of those cavalrymen have sense enough to appreciate the opinion of such a soldier as my ex-adjutant,—some of them, mind you: I don't admit that all cavalrymen have sense enough to keep them out of perpetual trouble,—you came in for a hearty endorsement, and you'll probably be up before the next board for examination. Go and bone your Constitution, and the Rule of Three, and who was the father of Zebedee's children, and the order of the Ptolemies and the Seleucidae, and other such things that they'll be sure to ask you as indispensable to the mental outfit of an Indian-fighter." It was evident that the colonel was in joyous mood. But Alice was silent. She wanted to hear the letter. He would have handed it to Frederick, but both Mrs. Maynard and Aunt Grace clamored to hear it read aloud: so he cleared his throat and began:

"MY DEAR COLONEL,—

"Fred's chances for a commission are good, as the enclosed papers will show you; but even were this not the case I would have but one thing to say in answer to your letter: he should go back to his troop.

"Whatever our friends and fellow-citizens may think on the subject, I hold that the profession of the soldier is to the full as honorable as any in civil life; and it is liable at any moment to be more useful. I do not mean the officer alone. I say, and mean, the soldier. As for me, I would rather be first sergeant of my troop or company, or sergeant-major of my regiment, than any lieutenant in it except the adjutant. Hope of promotion is all that can make a subaltern's life endurable, but the staff-sergeant or the first sergeant, honored and respected by his officers, decorated for bravery by Congress, and looked up to by his comrades, is a king among men. The pay has nothing to do with it. I say to Renwick, 'Come back as soon as your wound will let you,' and I envy him the welcome that will be his.

"As for me, I am even more eager to get back to you all; but things look very dubious. The doctors shake their heads at anything under a month, and say I'll be lucky if I eat my Thanksgiving dinner with you. If trying to get well is going to help, October shall not be done with before B Company will report me present again.

"I need not tell you, my dear old friend, how I rejoice with you in your—hum and haw and this is all about something else," goes on the colonel, in malignant disregard of the longing looks in the eyes of three women, all of whom are eager to hear the rest of it, and one of whom wouldn't say so for worlds. "Write to me often. Remember me warmly to the ladies of your household. I fear Miss Alice would despise this wild, open prairie-country; there is no golden-rod here, and I so often see her as—hum and hum and all that sort of talk of no interest to anybody," says he, with a quizzical look over his "bows" at the lovely face and form bending forward with forgetful eagerness to hear how "he so often sees her." And there is a great bunch of golden-rod in her lap now, and a vivid blush on her cheek. The colonel is waxing as frivolous as Fred, and quite as great a tease.

And then October comes, and Fred has gone, and the colonel and his household are back at Sibley, where the garrison is enraptured at seeing them, and where the women precipitate themselves upon them in tumultuous welcome. If Alice cannot quite make up her mind to return the kisses, and shrinks slightly from the rapturous embrace of some of the younger and more impulsive of the sisterhood,—if Mrs. Maynard is a trifle more distant and stately than was the case before they went away,—the garrison does not resent it. The ladies don't wonder they feel indignant at the way people behaved and talked; and each lady is sure that the behavior and the talk were all somebody else's; not by any possible chance could it be laid at the door of the speaker. And Alice is the reigning belle beyond dispute, though there is only subdued gayety at the fort, for the memory of their losses at the Spirit Wolf is still fresh in the minds of the regiment. But no man alludes to the events of the black August night, no woman is permitted to address either Mrs. Maynard or her daughter on the subject. There are some who seek to be confidential and who cautiously feel their way for an opening, but the mental sparring is vain: there is an indefinable something that tells the intruder, "Thus far, and no farther." Mrs. Maynard is courteous, cordial, and hospitable, Alice sweet and gracious and sympathetic, even, but confidential never.

And then Captain Armitage, late in the month, comes home on crutches, and his men give him a welcome that makes the rafters ring, and he rejoices in it and thanks them from his heart; but there is a welcome his eyes plead for that would mean to him far more than any other. How wistfully he studies her face! How unmistakable is the love and worship in every tone! How quickly the garrison sees it all, and how mad the garrison is to see whether or not 'tis welcome to her! But Alice Renwick is no maiden to be lightly won. The very thought that the garrison had so easily given her over to Jerrold is enough to mantle her cheek with indignant protest. She accepts his attentions, as she does those of the younger officers, with consummate grace. She shows no preference, will grant no favors. She makes fair distribution of her dances at the hops at the fort and the parties in town. There are young civilians who begin to be devoted in society and to come out to the fort on every possible opportunity, and these, too, she welcomes with laughing grace and cordiality. She is a glowing, radiant, gorgeous beauty this cool autumn, and she rides and drives and dances, and, the women say, flirts, and looks handsomer every day, and poor Armitage is beginning to look very grave and depressed. "He wooes and wins not," is the cry. His wound has almost healed, so far as the thigh is concerned, and his crutches are discarded, but his heart is bleeding, and it tells on his general condition. The doctors say he ought to be getting well faster, and so they tell Miss Renwick,—at least somebody does; but still she relents not, and it is something beyond the garrison's power of conjecture to decide what the result will be. Into her pretty white-and-yellow room no one penetrates except at her invitation, even when the garrison ladies are spending the day at the colonel's; and even if they did there would be no visible sign by which they could judge whether his flowers were treasured or his picture honored above others. Into her brave and beautiful nature none can gaze and say with any confidence either "she loves" or "she loves not." Winter comes, with biting cold and blinding snow, and still there is no sign. The joyous holidays, the glad New Year, are almost at hand, and still there is no symptom of surrender. No one dreams of the depth and reverence and gratitude and loyalty and strength of the love that is burning in her heart until, all of a sudden, in the most unexpected and astonishing way, it bursts forth in sight of all.

They had been down skating on the slough, a number of the youngsters and the daughters of the garrison. Rollins was there, doing the devoted to Mamie Gray, and already there were gossips whispering that she would soon forget she ever knew such a beau as Jerrold in the new-found happiness of another one; Hall was there with the doctor's pretty daughter, and Mrs. Hoyt was matronizing the party, which would, of course, have been incomplete without Alice. She had been skating hand in hand with a devoted young subaltern in the artillery, and poor Armitage, whose leg was unequal to skating, had been ruefully admiring the scene. He had persuaded Sloat to go out and walk with him, and Sloat went; but the hollow mockery of the whole thing became apparent to him after they had been watching the skaters awhile, and he got chilled and wanted Armitage to push ahead. The captain said he believed his leg was too stiff for further tramping and would be the better for a rest; and Sloat left him.

Heavens! how beautiful she was, with her sparkling eyes and radiant color, glowing with the graceful exercise! He sat there on an old log, watching the skaters as they flew by him, and striving to keep up an impartial interest, or an appearance of it, for the other girls. But the red sun was going down, and twilight was on them all of a sudden, and he could see nothing but that face and form. He closed his eyes a moment to shut out the too eager glare of the glowing disk taking its last fierce peep at them over the western bluffs, and as he closed them the same vision came back,— the picture that had haunted his every living, dreaming moment since the beautiful August Sunday in the woodland lane at Sablon. With undying love, with changeless passion, his life was given over to the fair, slender maiden he had seen in all the glory of the sunshine and the golden-rod, standing with uplifted head, with all her soul shining in her beautiful eyes and thrilling in her voice. Both worshipping and worshipped was Alice Renwick as she sang her hymn of praise in unison with the swelling chorus that floated through the trees from the little brown church upon the hill. From that day she was Queen Alice in every thought, and he her loyal, faithful knight for weal or woe.

Boom went the sunset gun far up on the parade above them. 'Twas dinner-time, and the skaters were compelled to give up their pastime. Armitage set his teeth at the entirely too devotional attitude of the artilleryman as he slowly and lingeringly removed her skates, and turned away in that utterly helpless frame of mind which will overtake the strongest men on similar occasions. He had been sitting too long in the cold, and was chilled through and stiff, and his wounded leg seemed numb. Leaning heavily on his stout stick, he began slowly and painfully the ascent to the railway, and chose for the purpose a winding path that was far less steep, though considerably longer, than the sharp climb the girls and their escorts made so light of. One after another the glowing faces of the fair skaters appeared above the embankment, and their gallants carefully convoyed them across the icy and slippery track to the wooden platform beyond. Armitage, toiling slowly up his pathway, heard their blithe laughter, and thought with no little bitterness that it was a case of "out of sight out of mind" with him, as with better men. What sense was there in his long devotion to her? Why stand between her and the far more natural choice of a lover nearer her years? "Like unto like" was Nature's law. It was flying in the face of Providence to expect to win the love of one so young and fair, when others so young and comely craved it. The sweat was beaded on his forehead as he neared the top and came in sight of the platform. Yes, they had no thought for him. Already Mrs. Hoyt was half-way up the wooden stairs, and the others were scattered more or less between that point and the platform at the station. Far down at the south end paced the fur-clad sentry. There it was an easy step from the track to the boards, and there, with much laughter but no difficulty, the young officers had lifted their fair charges to the walk. All were chatting gayly as they turned away to take the wooden causeway from the station to the stairs, and Miss Renwick was among the foremost at the point where it left the platform. Here, however, she glanced back and then about her, and then, bending down, began fumbling at the buttons of her boot.

"Oh, permit me, Miss Renwick," said her eager escort. "I

will button it."

"Thanks, no. Please don't wait, good people. I'll be with you in an instant."

And so the other girls, absorbed in talk with their respective gallants, passed her by, and then Alice Renwick again stood erect and looked anxiously but quickly back.

"Captain Armitage is not in sight, and we ought not to leave him. He may not find it easy to climb to that platform," she said.

"Armitage? Oh, he'll come on all right," answered the batteryman, with easy assurance. "Maybe he has gone round by the road. Even if he hasn't, I've seen him make that in one jump many a time. He's an active old buffer for his years."

"But his wound may prove too much for that jump now. Ah there he comes," she answered, with evident relief; and just at the moment, too, the forage-cap of the tall soldier rose slowly into view some distance up the track, and he came walking slowly down on the sharp curve towards the platform, the same sharp curve continuing on out of sight behind him,—behind the high and rocky bluff.

"He's taken the long way up," said the gunner. "Well, shall we go on?"

"Not yet," she said, with eyes that were glowing strangely and a voice that trembled. Her cheeks, too, were paling. "Mr. Stuart, I'm sure I heard the roar of a train echoed back from the other side."

"Nonsense, Miss Renwick! There's no train either way for two hours yet."

But she had begun to edge her way back toward the platform, and he could not but follow. Looking across the intervening space,—a rocky hollow twenty feet in depth,—he could see that the captain had reached the platform and was seeking for a good place to step up; then that he lifted his right foot and placed it on the planking and with his cane and the stiff and wounded left leg strove to push himself on. Had there been a hand to help him, all would have been easy enough; but there was none, and the plan would not work. Absorbed in his efforts, he could not see Stuart; he did not see that Miss Renwick had left her companions and was retracing her steps to get back to the platform. He heard a sudden dull roar from the rocks across the stream; then a sharp, shrill whistle just around the bluff. My God! a train, and that man there, alone, helpless, deserted! Stuart gave a shout of agony: "Back! Roll back over the bank!" Armitage glanced around; determined; gave one mighty effort; the iron-ferruled stick slipped on the icy track, and down he went, prone between the glistening rails, even as the black vomiting monster came thundering round the bend. He had struck his head upon the iron, and was stunned, not senseless, but scrambled to his hands and knees and strove to crawl away. Even as he did so he heard a shriek of anguish in his ears, and with one wild leap Alice Renwick came flying from the platform in the very face of advancing death, and the next instant, her arm clasped about his neck, his strong arms tightly clasping *her*, they were lying side by side, bruised, stunned, but safe, in a welcoming snow-drift half-way down the hither bank.

When Stuart reached the scene, as soon as the engine and some wrecking-cars had thundered by, he looked down upon a picture that dispelled any lingering doubt in his mind. Armitage, clasping Queen Alice to his heart, was half rising from the blessed mantlet of the snow, and she, her head upon his broad shoulder, was smiling faintly up into his face: then the glorious eyes closed in a death-like swoon.

*　　*　　*　　*　　*

Fort Sibley had its share of sensations that eventful year. Its crowning triumph in the one that followed was the wedding in the early spring. Of all the lovely women there assembled, the bride by common consent stood unrivalled,—Queen Alice indeed. There was some difference of opinion among authorities as to who was really the finest-looking and most soldierly among the throng of officers in the conventional full-dress uniform: many there were who gave the palm to the tall, dark, slender lieutenant of cavalry who wore his shoulder-knots for the first time on this occasion, and who, for a man from the ranks, seemed consummately at home in the manifold and trying duties of a groomsman. Mrs. Maynard, leaning on his arm at a later hour and looking up rapturously in his bronzed features, had no divided opinion. While others had by no means so readily forgotten or forgiven the mad freak that so nearly involved them all in wretched misunderstanding, she had nothing but rejoicing in his whole career. Proud of the gallant officer who had won the daughter whom she loved so tenderly, she still believes, in the depths of the boundless mother-love, that no man can quite surpass her soldier son.

[Footnote A: By act of Congress, officers may be addressed by the title of the highest rank held by them in the volunteer service during the war. The colonel always punctiliously so addressed his friend and subordinate, although in the army his grade was simply that of first lieutenant.]

Choose from Thousands of 1stWorldLibrary Classics By

A. M. Barnard
Ada Leverson
Adolphus William Ward
Aesop
Agatha Christie
Alexander Aaronsohn
Alexander Kielland
Alexandre Dumas
Alfred Gatty
Alfred Ollivant
Alice Duer Miller
Alice Turner Curtis
Alice Dunbar
Allen Chapman
Alleyne Ireland
Ambrose Bierce
Amelia E. Barr
Amory H. Bradford
Andrew Lang
Andrew McFarland Davis
Andy Adams
Angela Brazil
Anna Alice Chapin
Anna Sewell
Annie Besant
Annie Hamilton Donnell
Annie Payson Call
Annie Roe Carr
Annonaymous
Anton Chekhov
Archibald Lee Fletcher
Arnold Bennett
Arthur C. Benson
Arthur Conan Doyle
Arthur M. Winfield
Arthur Ransome
Arthur Schnitzler
Arthur Train
Atticus
B.H. Baden-Powell
B. M. Bower
B. C. Chatterjee
Baroness Emmuska Orczy
Baroness Orczy
Basil King
Bayard Taylor
Ben Macomber
Bertha Muzzy Bower
Bjornstjerne Bjornson

Booth Tarkington
Boyd Cable
Bram Stoker
C. Collodi
C. E. Orr
C. M. Ingleby
Carolyn Wells
Catherine Parr Traill
Charles A. Eastman
Charles Amory Beach
Charles Dickens
Charles Dudley Warner
Charles Farrar Browne
Charles Ives
Charles Kingsley
Charles Klein
Charles Hanson Towne
Charles Lathrop Pack
Charles Romyn Dake
Charles Whibley
Charles Willing Beale
Charlotte M. Braeme
Charlotte M. Yonge
Charlotte Perkins Stetson
Clair W. Hayes
Clarence Day Jr.
Clarence E. Mulford
Clemence Housman
Confucius
Coningsby Dawson
Cornelis DeWitt Wilcox
Cyril Burleigh
D. H. Lawrence
Daniel Defoe
David Garnett
Dinah Craik
Don Carlos Janes
Donald Keyhoe
Dorothy Kilner
Dougan Clark
Douglas Fairbanks
E. Nesbit
E. P. Roe
E. Phillips Oppenheim
E. S. Brooks
Earl Barnes
Edgar Rice Burroughs
Edith Van Dyne
Edith Wharton

Edward Everett Hale
Edward J. O'Biren
Edward S. Ellis
Edwin L. Arnold
Eleanor Atkins
Eleanor Hallowell Abbott
Eliot Gregory
Elizabeth Gaskell
Elizabeth McCracken
Elizabeth Von Arnim
Ellem Key
Emerson Hough
Emilie F. Carlen
Emily Bronte
Emily Dickinson
Enid Bagnold
Enilor Macartney Lane
Erasmus W. Jones
Ernie Howard Pie
Ethel May Dell
Ethel Turner
Ethel Watts Mumford
Eugene Sue
Eugenie Foa
Eugene Wood
Eustace Hale Ball
Evelyn Everett-green
Everard Cotes
F. H. Cheley
F. J. Cross
F. Marion Crawford
Fannie E. Newberry
Federick Austin Ogg
Ferdinand Ossendowski
Fergus Hume
Florence A. Kilpatrick
Fremont B. Deering
Francis Bacon
Francis Darwin
Frances Hodgson Burnett
Frances Parkinson Keyes
Frank Gee Patchin
Frank Harris
Frank Jewett Mather
Frank L. Packard
Frank V. Webster
Frederic Stewart Isham
Frederick Trevor Hill
Frederick Winslow Taylor

Friedrich Kerst
Friedrich Nietzsche
Fyodor Dostoyevsky
G.A. Henty
G.K. Chesterton
Gabrielle E. Jackson
Garrett P. Serviss
Gaston Leroux
George A. Warren
George Ade
Geroge Bernard Shaw
George Cary Eggleston
George Durston
George Ebers
George Eliot
George Gissing
George MacDonald
George Meredith
George Orwell
George Sylvester Viereck
George Tucker
George W. Cable
George Wharton James
Gertrude Atherton
Gordon Casserly
Grace E. King
Grace Gallatin
Grace Greenwood
Grant Allen
Guillermo A. Sherwell
Gulielma Zollinger
Gustav Flaubert
H. A. Cody
H. B. Irving
H.C. Bailey
H. G. Wells
H. H. Munro
H. Irving Hancock
H. R. Naylor
H. Rider Haggard
H. W. C. Davis
Haldeman Julius
Hall Caine
Hamilton Wright Mabie
Hans Christian Andersen
Harold Avery
Harold McGrath
Harriet Beecher Stowe
Harry Castlemon
Harry Coghill
Harry Houidini

Hayden Carruth
Helent Hunt Jackson
Helen Nicolay
Hendrik Conscience
Hendy David Thoreau
Henri Barbusse
Henrik Ibsen
Henry Adams
Henry Ford
Henry Frost
Henry James
Henry Jones Ford
Henry Seton Merriman
Henry W Longfellow
Herbert A. Giles
Herbert Carter
Herbert N. Casson
Herman Hesse
Hildegard G. Frey
Homer
Honore De Balzac
Horace B. Day
Horace Walpole
Horatio Alger Jr.
Howard Pyle
Howard R. Garis
Hugh Lofting
Hugh Walpole
Humphry Ward
Ian Maclaren
Inez Haynes Gillmore
Irving Bacheller
Isabel Cecilia Williams
Isabel Hornibrook
Israel Abrahams
Ivan Turgenev
J.G.Austin
J. Henri Fabre
J. M. Barrie
J. M. Walsh
J. Macdonald Oxley
J. R. Miller
J. S. Fletcher
J. S. Knowles
J. Storer Clouston
J. W. Duffield
Jack London
Jacob Abbott
James Allen
James Andrews
James Baldwin

James Branch Cabell
James DeMille
James Joyce
James Lane Allen
James Lane Allen
James Oliver Curwood
James Oppenheim
James Otis
James R. Driscoll
Jane Abbott
Jane Austen
Jane L. Stewart
Janet Aldridge
Jens Peter Jacobsen
Jerome K. Jerome
Jessie Graham Flower
John Buchan
John Burroughs
John Cournos
John F. Kennedy
John Gay
John Glasworthy
John Habberton
John Joy Bell
John Kendrick Bangs
John Milton
John Philip Sousa
John Taintor Foote
Jonas Lauritz Idemil Lie
Jonathan Swift
Joseph A. Altsheler
Joseph Carey
Joseph Conrad
Joseph E. Badger Jr
Joseph Hergesheimer
Joseph Jacobs
Jules Vernes
Julian Hawthrone
Julie A Lippmann
Justin Huntly McCarthy
Kakuzo Okakura
Karle Wilson Baker
Kate Chopin
Kenneth Grahame
Kenneth McGaffey
Kate Langley Bosher
Kate Langley Bosher
Katherine Cecil Thurston
Katherine Stokes
L. A. Abbot
L. T. Meade

L. Frank Baum
Latta Griswold
Laura Dent Crane
Laura Lee Hope
Laurence Housman
Lawrence Beasley
Leo Tolstoy
Leonid Andreyev
Lewis Carroll
Lewis Sperry Chafer
Lilian Bell
Lloyd Osbourne
Louis Hughes
Louis Joseph Vance
Louis Tracy
Louisa May Alcott
Lucy Fitch Perkins
Lucy Maud Montgomery
Luther Benson
Lydia Miller Middleton
Lyndon Orr
M. Corvus
M. H. Adams
Margaret E. Sangster
Margret Howth
Margaret Vandercook
Margaret W. Hungerford
Margret Penrose
Maria Edgeworth
Maria Thompson Daviess
Mariano Azuela
Marion Polk Angellotti
Mark Overton
Mark Twain
Mary Austin
Mary Catherine Crowley
Mary Cole
Mary Hastings Bradley
Mary Roberts Rinehart
Mary Rowlandson
M. Wollstonecraft Shelley
Maud Lindsay
Max Beerbohm
Myra Kelly
Nathaniel Hawthrone
Nicolo Machiavelli
O. F. Walton
Oscar Wilde

Owen Johnson
P.G. Wodehouse
Paul and Mabel Thorne
Paul G. Tomlinson
Paul Severing
Percy Brebner
Percy Keese Fitzhugh
Peter B. Kyne
Plato
Quincy Allen
R. Derby Holmes
R. L. Stevenson
R. S. Ball
Rabindranath Tagore
Rahul Alvares
Ralph Bonehill
Ralph Henry Barbour
Ralph Victor
Ralph Waldo Emmerson
Rene Descartes
Ray Cummings
Rex Beach
Rex E. Beach
Richard Harding Davis
Richard Jefferies
Richard Le Gallienne
Robert Barr
Robert Frost
Robert Gordon Anderson
Robert L. Drake
Robert Lansing
Robert Lynd
Robert Michael Ballantyne
Robert W. Chambers
Rosa Nouchette Carey
Rudyard Kipling
Saint Augustine
Samuel B. Allison
Samuel Hopkins Adams
Sarah Bernhardt
Sarah C. Hallowell
Selma Lagerlof
Sherwood Anderson
Sigmund Freud
Standish O'Grady
Stanley Weyman
Stella Benson
Stella M. Francis

Stephen Crane
Stewart Edward White
Stijn Streuvels
Swami Abhedananda
Swami Parmananda
T. S. Ackland
T. S. Arthur
The Princess Der Ling
Thomas A. Janvier
Thomas A Kempis
Thomas Anderton
Thomas Bailey Aldrich
Thomas Bulfinch
Thomas De Quincey
Thomas Dixon
Thomas H. Huxley
Thomas Hardy
Thomas More
Thornton W. Burgess
U. S. Grant
Upton Sinclair
Valentine Williams
Various Authors
Vaughan Kester
Victor Appleton
Victor G. Durham
Victoria Cross
Virginia Woolf
Wadsworth Camp
Walter Camp
Walter Scott
Washington Irving
Wilbur Lawton
Wilkie Collins
Willa Cather
Willard F. Baker
William Dean Howells
William le Queux
W. Makepeace Thackeray
William W. Walter
William Shakespeare
Winston Churchill
Yei Theodora Ozaki
Yogi Ramacharaka
Young E. Allison
Zane Grey

www.ingramcontent.com/pod-product-compliance
Lightning Source LLC
Chambersburg PA
CBHW050041180626
46810CB00002B/842